W9-ACH-118

.A TARGUM PRESS BOOK

6 diaries

six teens take a new look at tznius

First published 2009
Copyright © 2009 by Targum Press
ISBN 978-1-56871-513-1

All rights reserved

No part of this publication may be translated, reproduced, stored in
a retrieval system, or transmitted in any form or by any means, elec-
tronic, mechanical, photocopying, recording, or otherwise, without
prior permission in writing from both the copyright holder and the
publisher.

Published and distributed by:
TARGUM PRESS, INC.
22700 W. Eleven Mile Rd.
Southfield, MI 48034
E-mail: targum@targum.com
Fax: 888-298-9992
www.targum.com

Distributed by:
FELDHEIM PUBLISHERS
208 Airport Executive Park
Nanuet, NY 10954

Printed in Israel by Chish

Icon illustrations by Miri Weinreb

· · · · · · · · · · · · · · · · ·

To my mother,
who was my first and remains
my foremost role model of how
one can dress and act *b'tznius*
without compromising on
beauty or style.

· · · · · · · · · · · · · · · ·

A letter of approbation from Mrs. Zlata Press, Principal of Prospect Park Bnos Leah High School

Mrs. Goldin's book, *Six Diaries*, based on hours of frank conversation with her high school students, is an outstanding contribution to the question of how to best inculcate in our daughters and students the value of *tznius*.

These conversations bring to life the two fundamental principles which should lie at the heart of our *chinuch* efforts.

1. Our *talmidos* want us to recognize that they themselves value *tznius* and are struggling to find a way to live this value in a difficult environment.

2. Our *talmidos* must work through their own questions and difficulties so that they own the value which emerges. Our inspiring speeches and our critical glances have a short-lived effect. The process Mrs. Goldin describes transforms lives.

Is the book frank? Yes.

But truth permeates every page, as does, ultimately, the value and long-lasting effectiveness of this approach.

Thank you, Mrs. Goldin for your wisdom in guiding these conversations and thank you to your students and Targum Press for the courage to go public with them.

Zlata Press
Tammuz 5769

A letter of approbation from Rebbetzin Lea Feldman, internationally renowned educator

In today's confusing world, the beautiful mitzvah of *tznius* is often poorly understood. Girls feel like it's a burden rather than a gift. I have had the pleasure of reading *Six Diaries*, and I believe that it can do much to help bring teenagers to a better understanding and appreciation of *tznius*.

Using the true diaries of an exceptional group of high school students, the book takes a good look at the *hashkafah* that underlies *tznius*, how it permeates every aspect of our lives, and its transformative power. You hear the girls' voices, share in their struggles, and applaud their victories. All along the way, there are lessons to be gleaned.

This is a book for every girl who has grappled with *tznius*, for every parent and teacher who has groped for a way to transmit the fundamentals of this crucial mitzvah to the next generation. *Six Diaries* will be illuminating to the individual and thought-provoking to the group. It will stimulate class discussions and create an atmosphere in which *tznius* and spiritual growth are synonymous. No matter the setting or the format, *Six Diaries* will provide inspiration for every girl and woman.

Rebbetzin Lea Feldman
Tammuz 5769

Contents

ACKNOWLEDGMENTS

'd like to thank the following people who have all been an integral part of *Six Diaries.*

To all those who initially heard the idea and expressed such a strong interest in the book, particularly Bassi Gruen and Avigail Sharer of Targum Press, both of whom were a pleasure to work with.

To C. B., who was involved with this idea since its conception and reassured me constantly when I didn't know exactly which way the project was going with, "Don't worry, you never really know what you're doing..." Your friendship and advice is invaluable.

To my co-workers in the teachers' room, R. S. and L. L., for endless sessions of guidance in how to present certain ideas, and what to focus on, and when to let go...and for allowing me to call them five times a night for clarifications.

To Mrs. Press, for giving so generously of your time to explain concepts, take me back to the sources, and sharing your unique and refreshing approach to *chinuch habanos* in general. Although I graduated over a decade ago, Prospect Park continues to have a tremendous impact on my life in many ways.

To L. S. for showing me from the beginning what a kid can become. And for sharing, even when you really didn't want to.

To M. F. who spent endless hours helping me type the entries, and who should've been one of the original ten. I know I can always count on you to keep me in line.

To Gila Manolson, author of *Outside, Inside*, and Mrs. Chany Feldbrand, creator of the Ateres program. I've never met either one, but both had a tremendous influence on how I see the concept of *tznius*, and how I present it.

To my mother-in-law, whose constant enthusiasm and encouragement means so much to me.

And of course, to the original ten (well, eleven, but who's counting). It was you who kept me going, and who continues to inspire me with your strength, honesty, and courage.

May all of our efforts in the area of *tznius* be *mekadesh shem Shamayim*.

A. G.
5759/2009

INTRODUCTION

Last September, I approached ten girls and asked them if they would be willing to participate in a year-long project — an experiment, really. It was somewhat of a trial run: to find a way to teach *tznius* so that kids would understand that it means so much more than just clothing and school policy.

Kids in general are most receptive to the voices of their peers — one cool teenager can do (or undo) what fifty teachers hammer in using every teaching method available, and I wanted to tap into this. I also wanted to get the kids' take on *tznius* — what turned them on to the ideas? What turned them off? Where did *tznius* fit into their lives, and what role did it play when making the crucial small choices of their everyday realities?

The truth is, that I never imagined it turning out the way it did. I hoped to present a difficult topic in a way that girls would be receptive to it. I hoped that they would grow with each other and inspire each other to reach levels that they couldn't attain on their own. I hoped that the journals, which are the basis of this book, would be honest and open and, while I didn't take writing ability into account when selecting the girls, I hoped that their writing would be clear and easy to read.

I got all that — and more.

There is no more important topic to get across properly to a Jewish teenage girl than *tznius*, especially in the times we live in. And there is no topic more misunderstood and resented by teenage girls — and I'm sure that's not a coincidence. I wanted the girls to have a chance, to give them the facts on the ground before they made any assumptions about what *tznius* is or isn't. And I wanted to give parents and teachers a window into the minds of their girls. Because sometimes when we see a kid who's not measuring up, it's not even the kid's fault — it's we who are doing everything all wrong.

After ten years of teaching and talking to kids, I felt — to quote Avigail's journal — that Jewish teenage girls, even the *frum* ones, were being cheated out of something that is rightfully theirs. It's their inheritance, passed down lovingly by generations of women before them, sometimes at great sacrifice.

So this book is for my students — all of them. And it's for every kid who occasionally thinks that there's gotta be more to this *tznius* thing than what they've gotten so far. And it's for every Jewish woman and girl out there who is ready to be blown away by the power of a group of kids who decide to focus their energies enough to allow them to fly.

● ● ●

The girls who wrote this book were chosen from all four grades of high school, from different groups of friends and levels of *frumkeit*. I wanted a cross-section of *frum* kids, not ten clones. I also didn't want kids who knew each other well. While that made for slightly awkward beginnings, it allowed them to be completely honest without being held back by the thought, *what are my friends thinking about me right now?*

The girls would each have to attend one after-school meeting a month, where we would explore different topics in *tznius* together, and they would have to be willing to discuss anything and everything within the group completely openly. In addition, each girl would be given a journal in which she had to record all of her thoughts connected with the topics we were discussing, as well as anything else going on in her life that she felt was relevant. About once every two weeks, I would write the group a note with different topic starters, questioning what they thought about different issues in *tznius* that I felt were relevant to them. (I included these letters in an appendix.)

Avigail, Chavi, Rachel, Shevi, Ellie, and Sarah are all real high-school girls, and the journals you are about to read are actual entries. The names were changed, as well as certain telling facts about them, in order to protect their privacy.

I include a brief synopsis of what we spoke about at each month's meeting, though not every detail of the topics that were discussed. This book is not intended to be a collection of the *hashkafos* and *halachos* of *tznius*. There are some of those already out there (though not enough), and I am certainly not the one to write another. This book was intended to share the girls' personal reflections as they embarked and traveled on a year-long journey toward *tznius*. I hope their journals change your life even a fraction as much as they've changed ours.

NOTE TO READER

The girls who wrote the book you are about to read come from different backgrounds and different walks of life. While all six are Orthodox girls, all *shomrei Torah* and mitzvos to the best of their abilities, you are sure to find discrepancies between their *nisyonos* and yours. As they write about their issues with *tznius*, and the various things they are working on, don't get stuck on their individual examples. As you get to know the girls, you will be struck by the universality of their struggles, and you will find that their issues and your issues are really one. As Jewish girls struggling to make Hashem's will our own, we are all the same and we all fight the same battle to secure our identities. We are all sisters — daughters of the same King.

OCTOBER

Tznius — Again?

THE FIRST MEETING

The first time we all met was in October. The girls were all mildly self-conscious, and they sat stiffly around the table, waiting to be told what to do.

I began by telling the girls about the project. I had obviously asked them all to be a part of this whole thing, so they had an idea of what we were doing, but I knew they were still unclear about it. (At that point, to be honest, I was also slightly unclear about it.) So I set out to clarify. We — they — were going to write a book. The book would be about their experiences as they explored certain topics in *tznius*, and it would include entries from the journals they would keep to chronicle what I hoped would be a voyage of self-growth. I made it very clear that the purpose of this group was not to radically change the way anyone dressed. I didn't want them to feel attacked or get offended (there would be plenty of time for that later).

Repeating something I heard from Rebbetzin Braunstein, we began by speaking about the fact that, for some reason, *tznius* is an area in which there is no *kinas sofrim*. We have friends that are phenomenal in *tefillah*, in *chesed*, in *tzedakah* — and we're so jealous of them! We so badly want to be like them. But it's not like that with *tznius*. When we see someone who is on a high level, our reaction is more often: well, my family's not *makpid* like that. Or...well, if my father was a big rabbi, I would also have to dress like that — but he's not, so I don't (*baruch Hashem*).

Why is that? We know *tznius* is a good thing but...we don't want to look like that.

So we spoke about what *tznius* is not supposed to be: ugly, blending into the shadows, pulling a cloth over our heads...

As Gila Manolson says in her phenomenal book, *Outside, Inside*, *tznius* is a lost art. It's a delicate balance. The old "attractive, but not attracting" theory. We roll our eyes, but it's good stuff, that theory.

Before I got into anything too deeply, I asked them questions — more for my own curiosity than anything else.

What comes to mind when I say tznius?

- Hard
- Ugly
- *Frum*
- Tights
- Self-esteem
- Beautiful

(Well, *baruch Hashem* for the last two, anyway.)

What is your main nisayon in the area of tznius?

- Neckline
- Boys
- Short skirts
- Boys
- Tightness
- Boys

Well, that took me by surprise. I wasn't even sure what they meant by boys, but I was beginning to feel a bit over my head. I told them that boys were only a part of the reason we had to dress and act a certain way. The reaction was immediate:

"Are you saying you can't wear or do anything you want in front of girls?"

I swallowed. "No."

Instant pandemonium.

"Guys, let's leave this now, we're going to come back to it. One thing at a time."

What is the one thing teachers, rabbis, and speakers say to you which is an instant turn off?

- When they tell us that we are responsible for the next generation blah, blah, blah...
- When they tell us that we can't wear colors, that anything in style is wrong.
- When they talk about things we totally can't relate to.
- When they make us feel so guilty, like there's no hope.

So here was my list of do-nots. I'd do my best.

The crux of that first lesson: *tznius* is about the internal. At its core it's about getting in touch with your *neshamah*, and not allowing your external to outshine your internal. It's about getting in touch with who you really are and forcing other people to focus on that as well. It's about a totality of being, and that's a lifetime of work. All very deep concepts. I could tell the girls didn't entirely get what I was saying, but they understood its significance. That was fine with me, because let's face it — how many adults (myself included) really get this stuff?

The idea of *tznius* is not: being ugly, blending into the wallpaper, being painfully shy, dressing unattractively. *Tznius* should not be the refuge of the homely. When you see a true *tzanua*, you see true beauty. You see a woman who shines from the inside, out. Ever see a girl whose outside screams so loudly you wonder if they have any idea who they really are?

Is *tznius* really that important? I asked.

Tznius is the foundation of our lives as a *bas Yisrael*.

They all groaned. Well, I asked for that. I started over.

There is a concept that the more important something is in your *avodas Hashem*, the stronger the *yetzer hara* will attack. What do you find the hardest? That's where the most crucial work needs to be done.

→ Ask any girl what she finds the hardest roadblock in her *avodas Hashem*, and if she's honest, she will tell you: *tznius*. Isn't that a pretty good indicator?

The girls had a hard time with this. Why is *tznius* any more important than anything else? they protested. But they couldn't fight with the *yetzer hara* argument.

It's brought down that each mitzvah corresponds to a different part of the body. When a person's arm or leg gets infected, G-d forbid, he can still live without it. One can live without a limb. One can even live without both limbs, or all the limbs. It's a compromised life, to be sure, it's a life no one would envy, but it's still a life. But you can't live without a heart.

Tznius is the heart.

And that makes sense, because when it's done properly, *tznius* is not about one or another *eiver*. It's not about the knees, or the elbows, or the collarbone. *Tznius* is all-encompassing. It includes everything about you — what you wear, how you act, what you say.

The Vilna Gaon says that what Torah is to a man, *tznius* is to a woman. The girls were unimpressed. I wasn't worried, and continued developing this thought. This means, I told them, that if Torah is the fuel that feeds the man's *neshamah*, then *tznius* is the fuel that feeds the woman's *neshamah*.

If Torah is for every single male, then *tznius* is for every single female.

If the *yetzer hara* does everything in its power to stop a man from learning (in fact, the Chofetz Chaim used to say that the *satan* would be happy for a man to daven and say *Tehillim* all day, as long as he's not learning), then the *yetzer hara* will launch a similar attack to make sure the girl doesn't put the correct emphasis on *tznius*.

There was a collective blink.

This means that if a girl does *chesed*, if she davens, if she respects and honors her parents, and even loves to learn Torah, to a certain extent, the *satan* is pacified.

"Are you saying anything we do is worthless unless we're working on *tznius*?!"

"Are you saying all of the things we work on mean nothing?!"

"Are you saying all Hashem wants is our knees and elbows?!"

No, no, and no. I was just saying, the *satan* is somewhat pacified, because he got to keep the main thing.

Just like men have to toil and sweat for Torah, women have to toil and sweat for *tznius* ("literally," one girl said).

Just like Torah can be learned *shelo lishmah* in the beginning, so, too, *tznius* can be taken on *shelo lishmah*.

And just like Torah can only be fully appreciated when immersed in its world, so *tznius* can only be fully appreciated when immersed in its world.

It was a lot of information, most of which they had never heard before, and it was enough for one meeting. As they all packed up and left (pretty quietly), I was a little uncomfortable about the fact that I felt like I hadn't convinced them. Not that I was selling *tznius*, but it would have been nice if they had seemed more open to the ideas. As it was, I was feeling a lot of skepticism, and I was disappointed in myself that I couldn't do a better job of convincing them of *tznius'* inherent worth.

I stopped myself, though. This project was not about that. The point was not to convince them of anything, it was about getting down their thoughts as they work through these ideas. It was about giving them information, not ramming it down their throats.

In hindsight, I'm glad I didn't push too hard. At that point though, I was pretty unsure of where (if anywhere) we were headed.

• • •

♡ Avigail

I've pushed this off for a couple of days now, really because I have no clue what to write about. Obviously, something that has to do with *tznius* — but that's so general. *Tznius* is a *huge* topic, one that our school's always trying to get us interested in. Honestly, to me, all the speeches and classes say the same thing — basically, "just do it."

There are a billion questions I have on *tznius*, but even when I try to get the answers, nothing really clicks. Its not like I've never asked, though, or never read anything on the topic, because I have, I really have. That's why, when you asked me to be a part of this group, most of the appeal was in the fact that maybe I would finally understand *tznius*.

Guess I'll wait and see.

☆ Chavi

Ok, can I be honest for a second? Usually when I think about *tznius*, a few things come to mind — and none of them are too exciting. I'm not so good at it, it's not something I'm terrifically proud of. To me it means getting by in school, hoping that whatever needs to be covered is covered, and if not, then hoping I don't get caught. I know that's not what *tznius* is supposed to mean, and I'm open to hearing what it really is. It is extremely hard for me though, because I'm the type that hates when people label or stereotype. I think people would look at me differently if I changed the way I dressed. Maybe I will gain from this little group, maybe not. Only one way to find out...

(Sorry, but you told me to be honest.)

Rachel

So when I was on all these really inspirational summer programs (sorry, but I just had to jump right in) I was told so, so much about *tznius*. I heard so many things about how in order to become a better person, you have to start with your outside and stuff like that. Dress with *tznius*, and your actions will follow. But isn't that hypocritical? If we say that dress is an insight into who you really are, then how come so many girls dress perfectly, but really aren't all that great once you get to know them? Also, shouldn't you improve your insides before your outsides? Which is it?

I'm very embarrassed about this, but whenever I see a group of Bais Yaakov-type girls, and I see the whole all-black look, or the long-skirt, button-down shirt look, it makes me really nervous. Like, in a way, it scares me even to talk like them, because I'm afraid I'll end up dressing like that. Is that how you have to dress to be considered *tznius*? Why should our only creativity be in choosing the color of the stripes on our button-downs?

I have so many questions, which is funny because I think anyone looking at me would assume I'm totally fine with *tznius*. I know my clothing is really ok, but... I'm excited to be a part of this.

Shevi

So I'd say it's been about a week since you asked me to be a part of this whole group thing. I was happy, surprised, and really nervous all at the same time. I'm only in tenth grade, I'm not really sure I want to change all that much — I mean, I'm open to change I guess, I just... I don't know. But then I think of all the speeches from teachers and counselors about how they didn't change until they were out of high school, and how they always regret not doing anything about this stuff when they were younger...and it just got me thinking like — what am I waiting for?

As much as I learn about *tznius*, there are so many things that are hard for me. I really don't try to impress anyone, and honestly, my clothing is really not bad in terms of *tznius*. I grew up in a family that doesn't make *tznius* too hard — I mean, the basics are a given, and I'm for sure not the worst at *tznius* in my class or anything. But *tznius* is so much more than that — it's the way I speak, act, walk, laugh, the things I watch and listen to. I think that *tznius* really defines a girl, and maybe this group will help me become happier with who I am as a person.

I guess even if I only change a little, it would be worth it. I'm not looking at this as a way to change my life, but maybe it will help me sort out a few things.

♪ Ellie

Yeah, so this journal is really intimidating, I'm not gonna lie. And I don't really get why you chose me to be part of this... But, whether or not you end up using this, I think it will be a cool thing for me to do, so thanks!

Our first meeting is tomorrow. I don't even know the other girls in the group. The whole thing is so random.

I get frustrated sometimes — I hate when people judge me or my family. There are so many things about myself and my fam that I'm so proud of, and I hate when people act like clothing is the only thing that counts. I guess sometimes I ignore *tznius* because I think there are a lot of other really important things to work on. How come when someone tells another person that a girl got "*frummer*" over the summer, the first question is always, "What does she wear/not wear now?" That's so surface! There are so many ways of becoming "*frummer*" — more *kavanah* in *davening*, *shemiras halashon*, *kibud av va'eim*... Why is *tznius* always put first?

Sometimes when I'm working on myself (don't make fun), I push *tznius* aside in order to make this point — that internal stuff is more important. I tell myself that there are other things I need to work on, or that I'm not up to it yet.

Or maybe I just use that as an excuse to avoid the whole topic. Who knows?

Sarah

Tznius is one of those things in Judaism that no one really knows how to describe or how to talk about. It's a word that most kids want to just bleep out and not concentrate on — and I'm definitely one of those kids. I hate being told that something I'm wearing isn't good. I mean, doesn't everybody? I'm definitely open to growing and chang- ing...eventually. But honestly, I'm not looking to become a totally new person at this point in my life. So I think that these meetings are going to benefit me — maybe they'll actually tell me what *tznius* really is, and maybe if I understand it then I'll think about it more. Maybe I'll work on it because it's important to me as a Jew, and not just be- cause it's something I'm afraid of getting into trouble about in school. Maybe. Right now, I think of *tznius* as something I know I don't care about enough. Sometimes I feel bad because I know I *should* care, but other times I just feel like — what's the big deal, really?

Actually, that's a lie. I know it's a big deal, it's just really hard for me right now so I get defensive and say, Who cares about *tznius* anyway?

I do care. I just don't know why.

• • •

Avigail

Our first meeting is Monday after school. Chavi and I have been texting about it, we're trying to figure out what it's going to be about. You said you're not going to "*kiruv*" us into keeping *tznius* — I guess it's something you want us to come to on our own. I don't know how many perspectives of mine are going to change, though, because it's so hard for me. I mean, obviously I go to a *frum* school, and my house is all that also, but it's kind of forced on me. It's a struggle — what I'll do when my parents aren't watching, and what my mom calls "inner *tznius*." I do kind of understand the concept, but it's hard to accept. I know, it's all for our good, it protects us, brings us closer to Hashem, blah, blah, blah.

I have a friend that went off the *derech* a little while ago. She's not religious at all now, and she does everything you could think of wrong. Her *tznius* was the first to go — I watched it happen. She's still my friend. We're not so close, but we keep in touch. And while some people would, I guess, point her out as an example, it doesn't make me want to pull on knee socks or anything. Yeah, I definitely don't want to end up like her, but I think it just depends on where you draw the lines, you know? I'm not sure where my lines are. Not yet.

☆ Chavi

I've been thinking about our meeting for like the past two days. When I walked out of it, I felt like the worst person ever. I don't know if that's the point, but I feel like every session is just going to make me feel bad about myself. It's like the life I've lived so far is worthless because I've never really been so careful about *tznius* — which I recently found out is one of the defining, most important mitzvos. Am I supposed to feel this way? I don't know. I hope not, because I really hate it. I'm assuming it's just guilt...yeah, probably, but still, I don't want to change. I mean, don't get me wrong, I just...maybe I need to figure out who I really am.

Rachel

I was thinking about how when I'm dressed a certain way around certain types of people, I feel different than if I'd be wearing the exact same thing with a different group. Like, when I'm with my school friends, I feel cool dressing *frum* and I don't feel like a nerd at all. But when I'm with some kids I grew up with who don't go to my school, I always feel like I look so dumb — like there's no one there who's dressed at all like me.

I had a wedding last night — my *madrichah* from camp. She is always so *tznius*, and she like, radiated beauty. She loves Torah and inspired me constantly. She was the most beautiful bride I've ever seen — her inside so matched her outside. She's really my role model.

Shevi

Well, we finally met, and now I'm thinking about all these things. First of all, everything makes sense to me and I understand why *tznius* is so important, but it hasn't like...hit me yet. I'm still not totally getting it. I understand how *tznius* is taking attention off your external and focusing more on your internal, and that totally makes sense to me. But it's so hard — everyone wants to look good and, in a way, don't we all want attention? Also, I was just thinking that you can see what you look like on the outside, but you can't visualize your soul and you have no clue what it looks like. So you know you want it pure, and by being *tznius* it helps that, but it's just hard because you can't actually see it.

I also understand that *tznius* is the foundation of a *bas Yisrael*, but now what? Like, where is that thought supposed to take me?

Sometimes, I think that the *yetzer hara* must be really, really strong, because it really all makes sense and it's still so hard! I do want to be a more *tznius* person, I realize how important it is, but I'm not sure, there's something that keeps holding me back from actually doing anything more than I'm already doing.

♪ Ellie

After last night's session, I started thinking. I never realized how important *tznius* is really, and how many things fall under that category. Sometimes I think like, what does Hashem want from us already — to be perfect? Because I'll never get there. Sometimes I try really hard, but it's just not good enough. I just want to be close to G-d and be happy, but then I feel like He just keeps making it harder. Is this His way of making us stronger?

A couple of girls mentioned that they have major differences of opinion with their parents about this stuff, and they fight about it all the time. Thank G-d, me and my mom agree about how I should dress, and she's really not all that into it. I feel like I'm lucky and unlucky at the same time. Like, I'm glad I have the freedom to choose my clothes and grow on my own, but on the other hand, sometimes I feel like if she would have been stricter with me when I was younger, I wouldn't have the struggles I do now.

Did you know it's a lot harder to write all this personal stuff than spew for English class?

 Sarah

Inspiration is a strange thing. I mean, it's a nice thing to have in the world, but it's such a pain sometimes. You hear a really good speaker, or have a really deep convo with a friend, and you become Inspired. What does it mean to become inspired? It means hearing or seeing or thinking about something, and then wanting to connect with that thing.

Example: *tznius*.

So I go to camp, right? And all the girls and staff have their own struggles and stories and backgrounds. To me, camp is one of the most inspiring places on earth. I've made friends there who are older, and more experienced than me, girls who have chosen to be *frum* and *tznius* and "good," not because they're *rebbetzins*, but because their life experiences just caused them to change. Things happened to them, and they acted.

And that's the annoying part of inspiration — knowing that if you don't act on it, it will disappear.

So what's the moral of the story? I know for myself, something as hard to work on as *tznius* is going to take a lot of inspiration to lead me to action. It's not that I don't want to eventually, somewhere down the line, become a more *tzanua* person. It's just that in order for that to happen I'll have to learn how much I'm doing wrong and how bad I am now — how far away I am from that eventual person I want to become. Hate that.

● ● ●

♥ Avigail

I don't know where to start. We spoke about so many things at the meeting... I mean, it was good, but for some reason, even when I'm all inspired, nothing really changes. The effect of the moment wears off and I settle back into my circle of friends again. And then, whatever it is, peer pressure or just wanting to look good (which usually means covering less), I don't change anything.

I always wonder how my life would be different if *tznius* came easily. One thing's for sure, I would have a better relationship with my parents. There's always a fight between us on this. But, the more they try to push me to keep it, the more they turn me off. I think it's because of the way they do it. I just end up feeling like a horrible person — just because I don't have the same perspective as them. That's also a really big turnoff — like with speakers and teachers and stuff. They present a certain standard, like elbows or flashy colors, and they make it seem like that's what *tznius* is all about. And if you don't hold like them, you're going to burn for all eternity. They also distort the whole concept by just focusing on the collarbone, or whatever. That is not what being a *tzanua* is. You could be dressed in black from head to toe, and still walk a certain way, flipping your hair all over the place. Just because everything is covered, doesn't mean you're a *tzanua*.

☆ Chavi

Today I came to school in a long black skirt, tights, and the whole deal — but I felt like something was missing. I tried being extra careful with my language and behavior. I tried, but obviously not hard enough. The truth is, I don't really know what I'm trying <u>for</u>. I know I'm supposed to be a *tzanua*, have Jewish pride — and I do — but I don't really understand what it means to have my "outer" self reflect my "inner" self. If I don't know who I am, how could I be "in touch with my soul"? I don't think that putting on different clothes for a while will actually change me. In order to change permanently, you have to have the right intentions and goals while dressing a certain way. It's too easy to just throw on clothes and all of a sudden be a new person. I think it's a mental battle with yourself against society — people these days care way too much what people think. Either someone thinks it's too hard to be *tzanua* because society makes her feel ugly when she covers up, or she is not comfortable with her body in comparison to what society's standards are, so she takes refuge in dressing *tznius*. I'm not making sense.

I do want to change. I want to badly, but I just don't want to do it the wrong way and then possibly not be able to stick with it because I didn't start out properly. I think every decision with *tznius* should be thought out thoroughly and taken seriously.

🏵 Rachel

I had a Shabbaton this weekend and obviously I was staring at what everyone was wearing. I really couldn't understand why everyone was wearing such crazy short skirts. I wasn't judging them, but it made me think about past Shabbatons — I really don't think as many people wore such short stuff then. I don't want to judge anyone, but I really want to understand why. Is it because most clothing stores are only selling skirts that hit above the knee? Or just because they think it looks hot? Because to me, it's scary. How close are those dresses to being thigh-high? Like, where do they draw the line? I mean, when you use the knee as a guide then it's easy, because you can't pretend your knee is higher than it really is. Do they draw a line on their thigh and say, "Okay, higher than this I won't wear"? Unless there's a real line, it's just so risky.

🖋 Shevi

When I get dressed in the morning now, and I choose a tighter shirt or a shorter skirt, some things we spoke about come back to me. I put the not-so-good clothes back and choose something else, but it's really hard to find a skirt that covers my knees totally all the time.

♪ Ellie

This past summer, I became really good friends with a girl I met in camp. She's actually a lot *frummer* than me, but she's really awesome, and we spoke and hung out a lot. So one day, randomly, we decided to swap clothes for the day. I went to her closet, took a faded blue button-down, a classic Bais Yaakov flowy black skirt, put on tights, and stole her flats. Then I took a headband and made a poof and wore a low pony.

First of all, I really looked like her, it was kind of weird. Also, it was INSANELY hot that day, but omgsh, it was an awesome feeling. I wasn't committing myself to anything, so it wasn't scary or strange, it was just like a costume for a day, but it was really cool.

Then I had to take her into my bunkhouse. It took like fifteen minutes to find a skirt that was long enough and that she'd be willing to wear in public. She wore tights with my flip flops (don't ask), and a longer sleeve, higher neck shirt under a half-sleeve shirt I had there. It was really embarrassing. Over the summer, we were learning all this really awesome stuff, and everyone was improving and growing, and I was so excited to get to be wearing what I felt I couldn't wear, but should be wearing. And then I saw myself from someone else's perspective and saw how many basic things she needed to do before she would be willing to wear my clothes. It was depressing and totally flipped my mind. Then I realized that the whole thing had been my idea in the first place, possibly just so I could see myself exteriorly (is that a word?). I stole lots more of her clothes over that summer, and got rid of loads of my own. My suitcase home was a lot lighter than it had been in coming.

 # Sarah

So, we spoke about the different challenges everyone has and how some of us think that things like *lashon hara* are more important than *tznius*. Personally, I always thought that *shemiras halashon* is more important. Well, obviously, that's because I *know* how awful it can be, but I don't know enough about *tznius* yet. Also, *lashon hara* hurts people — it can hurt a lot of people all at once, and that hurt can't always be fixed. Doesn't a lack of *tznius* only hurt me? It's not that I don't care enough about myself — believe me, I'm self-centered when I need to be. It's just that it's easy for me to care about everyone else but me. It's easier to think about other people's hurt than the invisible pain I may be inflicting on myself. It's easier to focus on *lashon hara*, than on how much I need to improve in an internal area.

And *shemiras halashon* is a great thing to work on, after all. So it's not like I'm procrastinating exactly. I'm just focusing my improvement energies, or whatever. At least I'm trying to work on *something*. That way I don't feel bad about all the things I'm not working on. Like *tznius*.

• • •

♡ Avigail

Okay, so you told us to look in the mirror and write what we see.

I see the same face I've been seeing for the last fifteen years. There's also something else, though. I can't really explain it, but I'll try. When I see my reflection, sometimes I feel like I've been cheating myself of something that could be mine. I don't know what I mean. Some people would say that I'm talking about my potential. Maybe. Or is it who I really want to be inside?

That's it, I think. I feel like I'm being cheated out of who I really am. Not all the time, but often I know I portray someone who I'm really not. Why? Probably because it looks good.

I know that sounds shallow, but all relationships with teenagers are based heavily on exteriors. You could disagree, but we both know you'd be lying. So naturally, everyone wants to look their best. And it is very, very hard to pull off the button-down, long-skirt, low-ponytail look and still look beautiful.

There are some who do manage it, though. And they shine. I went to camp with one girl like that, she was from California. She keeps *tznius* to the utmost, but besides for that, she is just an amazing person. She always has a compliment, never speaks *lashon hara*, has the longest *Shemoneh Esrehs*...and what amazes me is that she doesn't even have to — no one's forcing her to, she came to it out of her own free will. She is insanely inspiring, and one of the only girls I can truly call a real *tzanua*. And that's amazing to me.

I know, though, that it will be a long, long time before I ever (if ever) come to her level. It's awesome to see though, how her outside is an exact reflection of her inside. I'm never sure if I match. There are times when I feel proud of myself, and of how I'm dressing. More often, I don't match though, because I feel like it looks good. But truthfully, I'm kind of embarrassed about those times. I know it's not who I am and that I'm giving off a shallow impression.

I truly do admire those girls who have enough courage to dress in a way that's *tznius*. The ones who are still dressed normal, but they cover up. Honestly, sometimes I think that looks a lot nicer than showing everything. To me it says "I have a body and it's not on display." At this point in my life, I just don't have that sort of willpower.

Until I truly understand *tznius*, it's going to be hard to totally accept it on myself. I mean, if you don't really, fully understand something, how can you accept it?

⭐ Chavi

So when I look in the mirror, I don't really take that deep of a look. It's like I see my face and what I look like, and that's about it. I can't say I'm always proud of the way I look, but whatever, I guess you learn to live with it. I don't really know, maybe I wear the clothing I wear to make me feel better about myself — doesn't everybody? Yeah, that doesn't really make a whole lot of sense, but the bottom line is, I don't really have the greatest self-esteem. So what I'm trying to say is that I just think that wearing the things that I imagine a *tzanua* wearing would make me feel *worse* about the way I look. I don't know if that's really clear or not, but those are my feelings in the clearest way possible.

❀ Rachel

I remember something one of my teachers said to my class about clothing. She was telling a story about how once, she had student over for Shabbos, and the student came down on Shabbos morning with a short skirt on. She described how the whole time, the girl was constantly tugging at her skirt, trying to keep it below her knees, and how she was always uncomfortable. The teacher wondered why she wore the skirt in the first place — if it tortured this girl so much! She was such a slave to her skirt that she couldn't enjoy Shabbos for what it was.

Lately, in my classes with men teachers I've become super sensitive to how much my legs show when I'm sitting down. But then I think, if I'm so uncomfortable that I have to drape a sweatshirt over my legs, then why do I wear this skirt in general?! So many girls are slaves to their clothing — but why...

✐ Shevi

I just have to write down a story that really inspired me. So my whole family was flying somewhere for a bar mitzvah, and at the airport they made us take off all our like...sweatshirts and stuff. And I was wearing a tee-shirt underneath, so I took mine off, but my sister would not budge because she wasn't comfortable with the length of her sleeves that she was wearing underneath. My sister's awesome. She's really funky but still *tznius*, and she makes me realize that it's possible to be both.

♪ Ellie

Okay, so everything sounds lovely, but really, I just don't think this is so practical. I won't say it's not for me, cause that's just stupid — if it's good for one person, then it's good for everyone. And I believe in gaining spiritual goodness, whatever, but is *tznius* really so up there on the priority list in heaven? What about things like *tefillah*, *simchah*, things like that? Call me a chassid, but I really feel like these things bring you close to G-d.

Also, it's not like I dress so badly, you know. If you have a choice of two mitzvos to work on, one which you're okay at and one which you stink at, which do you start working on first? Personally, I'd choose the latter. So I wear the skirts, pretty much at my knee, and shirts almost at my elbow, and I actually do cover my collarbone, for sure on school days. I honestly don't think I'm so bad.

And I happen to be *way* better than I used to be.

 # Sarah

I've noticed that it's not just the way I dress; it's the way I talk, too. I never really cared about my speech, 'cos I know I don't really use *really* bad words, at least not a lot. I mean, compared to my friends, I'm definitely the "*frummy*" of my group (which maybe says something about my group). The way I talk definitely depends on who I'm hanging out with. Also with my actions — the way I carry myself used to totally change based on who I happened to be with, but I made a conscious effort to stop being fake like that. It always bothered me when my friends — one kid in particular — would act differently around different people. Like around guys she'd be all giggly and weird, and then with teachers all *frum* and angelic. And with friends — ugh, I don't even know. And I just didn't want to be like that, you know? But my speech still...stinks, and my dress is not *tznius*, and I know it. But my actions — I think they're okay. Not great, but the best of the three I think.

So I've been thinking (dangerous, I know). *Tznius*, if you think about it, really is *cleanliness*, you know what I mean? Like, clean speech, clean dress, clean actions. It's genuine beauty. Pure, refined. And it sounds awesome when you say it like that, doesn't it?!

NOVEMBER

The Bigger Picture

THE SECOND MEETING

I started the second meeting the same way I did the first: What words come to mind when I say "*tznius*"?

- Difficult
- Clothing
- Refined
- Beauty
- Boys
- Self-confidence

(Well, I guess it was an improvement.)

The topic that I was going to discuss with them that night was one word that no one had written down: *kedushah*. *Tznius* — in actions, in dress, in thought — is the guardian of the *kedushah* in our lives. It is what allows Hashem's Shechinah to reside among us, it ensures our protection, and it is our destiny: "*V'atem tihiyu li mamleches kohanim v'goy kadosh.*" "ואתם תהיו לי ממלכת כהנים וגוי קדוש,"

The opposite of *tznius* is *pritzus*. *Pritzus* is a complete breakdown of *kedushah*. At best, *pritzus* is an overfocus on the body. At worst, it's an overfocus on immorality. And Hashem cannot be anywhere there is *pritzus*; it drives Him out completely.

The keys to *tznius* were given to women. We are the guardians of *kedushah*, and we are fighting the battle against *pritzus* on the front lines. *Kedushah* is not some esoteric concept belonging to *talmidei chachamim* residing in Bnei Brak. It belongs to everyone, and all Jews need to heed its call.

Then I addressed something I read in one of the journals: Why is *tznius* such a big deal — it only affects you. Isn't it worse to speak badly about someone — now, that really affects someone else? The fact is, though, that when you start seeing *tznius* as something bigger than the clothes you choose to wear; when you see it as protecting the *kedushah* which is an integral part of *klal Yisrael*, then you realize that your decision whether or not to be *tznius* at any given time is not a small, personal decision. It's huge. It's cosmic. It's global. We spoke about this thought from all angles, for a while.

There was also a topic that kept creeping up, both in our conversations and in their journals. It didn't surprise me, because teenagers tend to have very finely tuned antennae for hypocrisy. "So, someone that is so, so good in everything else, but who doesn't focus on *tznius*, Hashem is not with them?" And again: "What about all those people who dress so *tznius* but really they're so bad inside and they speak so much *lashon hara* and they don't daven or anything."

I was getting tired of constantly having to act as a lawyer for all the inconsistent Jews out there, the ones who are so great, but don't give a flip about the *halachos* of *tznius*. Or, the people who look like a poster child for *frumkeit*, but inside are nasty and mean. I didn't want to defend either group. Why couldn't the girls understand that we're all *people*? And, like all *people*, there are certain things that come easier than others, and we work on ourselves mitzvah by mitzvah. It's time to stop judging.

What's better, I asked the girls, to have your limbs intact, but to be attached to an artificial heart pump, or to be in a coma, lying there with a beating heart? Aren't they both lousy options? How many people are either one or the other, though? No one I know. We're all just doing the best we can, to greater and lesser degrees.

It was important to me that I convey the idea of the perfect balance. These girls have been getting too many messages telling them in one way or another that to be *tznius* is to blend in, to disappear, to be ugly and withdrawn. To them, *tznius* meant nerdy. I wanted to tell them that this isn't true, that we are supposed to be beautiful and fine and attractive looking. Who should be beautiful if not the daughter of the King?! So yes, *tznius* is often a list of things you cannot wear, but that doesn't take away from its positive aspects, from the fact that you should still be beautiful!

"What does Hashem want from us already?" the girls protested. "Now we have to follow all these guidelines and we're also expected to look beautiful all the time?!"

Obviously, something was getting lost in translation.

Next topic. I did want to address another area of supposed hypocrisy. There is often a thought that it is wrong to dress in a way which is inconsistent with one's level of *avodas Hashem*. As if to say, Who am I to dress this way? Who am I kidding?

✳ To clarify: hypocrisy is when one's actions are insincere, when we ✳ are trying to portray ourselves as something we are not. Hypocrisy is not when a person is yearning to be better, striving to reach a goal, stretching her limits. And this becomes especially applicable with *tznius*. If we would wait before taking on new levels, before covering the things we should and making the necessary adjustments to our wardrobes, well, most of us would still be sitting around, waiting to hear the Voice which would tell us "It's Time." There are kids who wait to be "up to it" before taking on certain levels of *tznius*. How many students go through four years of high school, and even through their year in Israel, and even into adulthood, all the while still waiting... We need to have a certain sense of *naaseh v'nishma* — first we will do. Sometimes, the beauty, the appreciation, comes after. And don't get dressed one morning in an outfit which is significantly more *tzanua* and expect the angels to sing. Sometimes, you have to create your own chorus.

This was not an idea that the girls took to easily. I had underestimated the power of an American upbringing, the antipathy toward doing something you don't understand completely just because someone tells you to. Even if that someone may be G-d Himself.

We ended off discussing the power of clothing specifically, and how it affects our mood and actions in a very real way. Sometimes we need to make a concrete change in the way we dress before we are able to realize how much our clothing has to do with our daily actions and attitudes. It doesn't benefit anyone to get stuck in the details and the sea of questions. You can start, even if the finish line is hazy in the distance (because it's a mirage).

It's not hypocritical, I told them. You're working on it. Just do it.

• • •

♥ Avigail

I definitely see how not keeping one part of a mitzvah can lead to a very bad chain reaction type of thing. I already told you about my friend who's not religious anymore — we hung out together at the mall recently. So, obviously I noticed all the changes in her — every other word that came out of her mouth was a curse word. She thought it was funny to trash stores and see how many she could get thrown out of, she's smoking like crazy now, and at one point I actually had to buy her a necklace to keep her from shoplifting it. When I asked her why she would do that, she said " 'Cause it's cheaper."

I know this is an extreme scenario, but it's also a reality. Our mitzvos *do* protect us, and I can see *tznius* as a key to those protective gates. I don't mean that we have to necessarily stay sheltered our whole lives and never do anything unless our parents tell us to. Mistakes definitely help us learn — as long as we do learn from them. And everyone makes them — I know I've messed up plenty of times. But I'm trying. And I can see which team I want to be on.

You don't have to be a perfect person to be a good one. Just as long as we want to be and do good — and I think we all want it at some level — it's okay. I guess we all just need the courage to act on that desire.

☆ Chavi

So I'm thinking back to a Shabbaton I went to last year around nowish. Back then, I didn't think about anything I did before I did it. I just wanted to have a good time and look cute. Really, I checked myself in the mirror about every twenty minutes to see if I still looked acceptable according to my standard of hotness. I was just always trying to put on a show for the guys — and even the girls, and yeah we were friends and did plenty of stupid things together. Since my parents weren't around that weekend, I totally dressed differently from the way I normally did and pretended that's who I was. I wanted everyone to think I wasn't as *frum* as I really was all the other days — except I think I *really* wasn't, because *frumkeit* is a mentality and I slipped away from it for a long weekend. I can see that now. And then, when the weekend was over, I kept in touch with all those kids, so in a sense, I got to pretend I was someone else for a long time.

It's sad how long it took me to realize how wrong it is to dress provocatively on purpose, or to pretend I'm not looking for all the attention and compliments, when really that's exactly what I craved. I convinced myself that there was nothing wrong with the way I stood or sat or laughed around certain people. It's sad when I realize how I wore my lip gloss, how I chose perfume, how I always had gum with me, wore makeup, took pictures on other people's phones.

I don't really believe in guilt. I am improving from where I was a year ago. I know I'm not perfect, and I never will be, but that doesn't mean I shouldn't strive for my best.

Rachel

Truthfully, whenever I think about being more *tznius*, I do want to, but I really can't go much farther. About three summers ago, I came home from a summer program, and literally did a 180 and dressed (and acted) totally differently. My family freaked out. I never heard the end of it. Between the "so now you're *chassidish*" comments and the "you think you're so great because you're dressed like that," it was really hard. I know I can never go to that extreme so quickly again. Once I started playing it down a little, it got better, but I still hear comments that I think I'm so good because I dress in a certain way.

Yeah, I know I shouldn't care what people think about the way I dress, and that the only thing that matters is "what Hashem wants" — that's all great, but what about when it really affects *shalom bayis*? I went through a miserable time then. It's so much better now, but I really could've used some advice at that point.

Sometimes I think, *Is that what I deserved for trying to be more tznius?*

Shevi

This past week I went to the Bais Yaakov convention. There were *tons* of schools there, and all of the girls in our group were told to wear button-down shirts with black sweaters, long black skirts, and tights. I was actually not so excited about it, because it's not the way I usually dress, but I knew it was the right thing to do at the time.

When I got there, I saw about fifty different uniforms. My first thought was, whoa, they actually have to wear that *every single day*?! Don't they feel like they get lost in the crowd? But after meeting a few of the kids, I realized that most don't feel that way at all. I started seeing them as individuals, not just a uniform. I realized that you don't have to fit a certain mold to dress in a *tznius* way. I'm not explaining it well, but this was really eye-opening for me.

I *can* dress in a way that makes me feel unique, while being *tznius*.

♪ Ellie

To tell you the truth, until this year, I didn't really spend any time thinking about *tznius*. I mean, I was pretty content with the level I was at. Not anymore. I want to accomplish more. Lately, I've been having a hard time connecting my *tznius* to the rest of my *ruchnius*. Like, I'm working on *kavanah*, and on my relationship with Hashem, and *chesed*, and all this other stuff. And I feel connected, inspired, etc. Then I think of *tznius,* and for some reason it seems completely separate from all that other stuff. Why is that? Why does *tznius* not inspire me? I mean, don't get me wrong, sometimes it does, like when I see someone who is a true *tzanua* in how she acts and carries herself, and she's still so, so beautiful...but it doesn't happen very often. You told us that first you work on it, then the feeling comes, so I'm going to try.

You know what else? In the first meeting, you were talking about how there's no *kinas sofrim* with *tznius*, but it's not true. I am sincerely jealous of some of the other girls in our group and their commitment to *tznius*. Like when Shevi was telling us about how she ripped up her skirt — that was insane! It's funny, you always assume that certain girls never have to work on *tznius*, like Shevi or Rachel, but they do. No matter what level a person is at, *tznius* always seems to be relevant.

Sarah

I have so much to write but I have *zero* time, it's *crazy*!

Ahh, okay so I'm going to start with Abercrombie bags, cuz I think it connects everything I've been thinking about lately. When I decide what bag I'm going to bring my gym clothes in to school or whatever, I admit my initial reaction is to reach for an Abercrombie or Hollister bag (which is, thank G-d, plain brown). Now, if I take the Abercrombie one I'll probably be carrying around a not-very-covered body most of the day. (Now, that's baggage...SNORT.) As I'm writing this, I'm laughing at my own stupidity. I inevitably end up carrying it in a way that the really bad picture faces me, so the whole world can't see it, because that's just awkward. But I wonder — if I'm aware of what I'm hiding, then why pretend I don't notice when I choose that bag to take? If you're so embarrassed of the picture, just take a different bag! No one said you have to be a walking brand-name ad 24/7!! And it's always been a fear of mine to meet a teacher that I really like and respect while I'm carrying one of the bad ones — well, any of them really. Cuz if I was trying to make a good impression, it wouldn't be so smart to shove Sedom and Amorah in their faces exactly.

And I think that that's the best example of dressing/acting in a way where your outsides don't match your insides. Inside, I'm a little embarrassed to be carrying around a bag with such a picture. Outside, I use the bag anyway. I think that, even though this sounds ridiculous even to me, I keep doing it, because I don't really know who I am on the inside. I don't know who I want my outside to reflect.

And *that's* a problem way bigger than which bag to carry around my gym clothes in.

● ● ●

♥ Avigail

The actual laws of the clothes have always been pretty easy for me. But I know I'm not following the actual spirit of the law. No, it doesn't say anywhere exactly how loose your shirt has to be, or exactly what kinds of words or pictures are allowed, so I take advantage.

I know that when I see a kid with a company's name plastered across her front, an iffy skirt, and tons of eye makeup, I don't think of her as extremely *tznius*. But when I see other kids who still can't do their own shopping and wait for mommy to tell them what to wear every morning, I just see them as robots.

There is a line between that, and I know it when I see it. It's these girls that are dressed *tznius* but cool, attractive but not flaunting, and they seem proud of it.

That's what I'm striving for — even though I know it's gonna take a while.

☆ Chavi

Sometimes I feel like the best way for me to learn how to be *tzanua* and still feel pretty is to look at pretty, *tzanua* people. It helps me because I see that unlike everyone else, they're not trying too hard. It's natural beauty that comes...naturally.

Tznius could have also saved me from a *lot* of moments in my life that I regret. It's always fun and crazy at the time, but looking back, when *tznius* goes, everything else follows.

❀ Rachel

So I was at the mall today, and I tried on a shirt that had this gather on top, and it was *so* cute, *and* it was on sale! I asked my mom if she thought it was pulling a lot on top and she said yes, so I sighed, put it back and walked away. I don't think that ever happened to me before.

Walking home from school yesterday, I stopped at a corner and saw three girls standing there in really tight jeans. One was like, swaying to the music, but very subtly. It sounds like nothing, but it was really, really provocative looking. There was no one there to act for — it's not like she was doing it intentionally, but people should be aware of how they look. We always act surprised and say, "OMG, I totally didn't mean to act that way! I can't believe that's how I came off!" As if that's an excuse.

Shevi

I've been meaning to write this for a while, but I just kept forgetting. I decided that I want to be extra careful with my *tznius* on Shabbos — like that my neckline and skirt length should be okay in the afternoon when I change. I'm gonna try it out and see what happens.

Saturday night, I went shopping and tried on a skirt that was just a drop too short and I didn't get it! I was really proud of myself! Also, that night I was more aware of my actions. I told my friend something *really* funny while we were walking, and we both started laughing like crazy, and I realized that *everyone* was staring at us. I got a hold of myself and thought of how we were talking about how people get crazy and hyper and pretend not to notice that everyone is staring at them. It's so true, though it's hard to recognize when you yourself are acting in a way that's not *tznius*.

Oh, here's something random that really bothered me. I was going with a whole group of friends to Six Flags one Sunday, and my friend's like, "Hey, what are you wearing?" So I'm like, "A jean skirt and long-sleeve shirt."

So then she goes, "Oh, I should've known. You're such a *frummy*." She was just kidding around, but it *really* bothered me. I didn't even know what to answer back.

Question: What about people who on the outside are all *frum* and nice-looking, but once you get to know them, they're really nasty people?

♪ Ellie

You know what I'm thinking? *Tznius* is sort of like cheating the system — like a shortcut. I'm finding that when I'm wearing a long black skirt or a good shirt (or both, would you believe?!), it's a lot harder for me to say something that's inappropriate, or even listen to something bad, and a lot easier for me to daven well, not say *lashon hara*, and just act better in general! I used to think that if I dressed in a certain way before I acted in a certain way, it would be wrong. I thought it would be like putting on a show and it wouldn't be for real — like giving off a wrong impression. I think that's just the *yetzer hara* though. Because really, *tznius* is a tool that makes doing the other mitzvos easier.

When we're wearing Shabbos clothes, it's easier to feel the *kedushah* of Shabbos. When I wear sweatpants under my skirt and a sweatshirt to school, it's a lot easier to fall asleep in class and act lazy through the rest of the day. *Tznius* is not just one mitzvah by itself, it causes a real chain reaction for everything else you do that day.

Sarah

So I'm thinking about how sometimes I feel better on the inside than I dress on the outside. Like I'm the type of person who davens with *kavanah*, and watches how I speak and all that, but I still wear tight shirts and short skirts, no socks and all that. We spoke a lot about how *tznius* and *pritzus* are opposites, and you can't have both. Either you're locking out Hashem, or you're letting Him in, and I definitely agree with that. I see it so clearly in my own life. When more of my body is covered, I definitely feel like more of my spiritual side can show, or whatever. I never thought I'd be saying that before we started these meetings, so I guess they've been affecting the way I *think*. As for the way I *dress*, I'm really not sure.

Sometimes I feel like I'm improving, and other times I know I'm not and I really don't care.

• • •

♥ Avigail

It happens to be that it all makes so much sense now. I know I still don't get everything, but right this second things seem much clearer. Hashem is our Father, and He does things we don't necessarily understand, and sometimes His reasoning might even be totally beyond our comprehension. But you know, that's okay.

I never understood *tznius*, and I never really wanted to, because then I'd just feel guilty for violating it. I kept myself back from growing.

It might be okay to not understand everything. Or anything. If I believe in G-d, that's okay. It's a crazy thought.

☆ Chavi

I realized something (good thing I have weekends so I can think about this stuff). When I get dressed for school, it's almost automatic that I pull a tanktop out of my drawer and put it on backwards so that the neckline will be okay. Well today (Sunday) I couldn't help but notice my neckline plunge a good four inches lower than any school day. I never would have thought about wearing a tanktop backwards outside of school — that's nuts. Anyway, that's a huge problem for me. I don't want to look like an idiot with the Hanes tag in the front, but at the same time I don't want to show what shouldn't show. Hmm...that's a brain buster.

Wait, another thing about the tanktop thing — I thought about why this never really bothered me before I started writing in the journal. I'm always convincing myself that it's okay my neckline is so low because that's where it falls on me — which is true. But I also ignore the fact that I keep buying these low-neck things, and not any other type of undershirt that would be higher. So the whole thing is not as passive as I thought. Okay, that's all I have to say about tanktops.

 Rachel

So I had my cousin's wedding, and my other cousin surprised her and flew in to be there. We had always been close growing up, and I was so happy to see her. We got along really well at first, but after a while it became so hard to talk to her. Everything she says and does comes off as so not *tznius*. She was a little like that when we were younger, too, but I kinda thought she would grow out of it. It makes no sense to me how someone who really is spiritual and tuned into her Judaism most of the time could not realize how not-*tznius* she acts. She happens to be a little large, so the shirts she wears might be fine on someone else, but on her they end up looking so...wrong. I hate saying this about her, because I really do love her, but everything she wore just looked so wrong and...cheap. Also, she has this sway when she walks, like superconfidence, if you know what I mean. I just don't get it. Her boundaries are really blurry, it makes me feel so uncomfortable.

I hate watching her like this. I keep telling myself not to judge her, but it really hurts me to see her throw this stuff away and not even realize what she's giving up.

Shevi

This morning I tried to do something for *tznius*, but it was really hard. I have this really cute jean skirt that's a little too short and it just sits in my closet and seriously I feel like my clothing can talk sometimes. It's like my head keeps telling me to wear it and my heart keeps telling me not to. Or maybe it's the opposite. Whatever.

I realized that there are a lot of people who are *tznius* but still dress really well. Like, I look around and see girls with the tight shirts and really short skirts — it doesn't even look good, it just lowers your value.

Sometimes when I'm sitting in class or somewhere else, I feel like I'm the outcast cos I'm the one wearing tights or a good neckline that day. But other times I kind of like that feeling. Like, it's kind of fun to be different like that — like I'm special because I'm *tznius*.

♪ Ellie

I have to admit that people dress the way they want to feel and act...

I was talking to a girl from a different school, and she was talking about maybe switching to a different one next year. She has friends there and likes the academics better, but the only thing holding her back is the dress code. She told me that if she has to walk around every day wearing longer skirts/sleeves and a higher neck, she might get used to it and change her way of thinking and acting, and she likes herself the way she is! This girl happens to be extremely honest about it. I don't think most people are.

I think the power of *tznius* might be stronger than most kids think — I think it can reconstruct someone's entire life. This girl understood that the way she's dressed during a few school hours, and then only because she *has* to, has the ability to change her as a person.

I didn't really agree with a lot of what that kid was saying or how she was thinking, but she was right in recognizing the power of dress.

 Sarah

I had three friends over for Shabbos, and a few more who walked over during the day, so *motza'ei Shabbos* there were like seven of us in my room trying to figure out what to do with ourselves. Obviously, the first thing we did was change into regular weekday clothes. So I pull out this shirt, and I don't even know *why* I ever got it — for a few reasons:

1. My first *kabbalah* when we started these meetings was not to wear shirts with brand names or other words printed across them. (The truth is, that was really my mother's *kabbalah for* me, but recently I adopted it as my own). This shirt (it's really cute) is a really nice green color, and has "Abercrombie and Fitch" printed in blaring white letters across the front with little gray and light blue A & F's all over it.

2. The neck is really low. I mean, it's not too bad if I keep pulling it up every once in awhile, but that basically means it's too low.

3. It's too tight. A few weeks ago that totally would not have bothered me, cuz it's not *that* tight (I've gotten rid of tighter ones, believe me), but now that I've really been trying not to wear shirts like that (which is *so* hard) it seems a lot tighter then it did before.

Anyway, I put on this shirt, and I'm wearing it with this cute skirt and cute shoes and my friends are all saying, "Omgsh, you look so good, blah, blah, blah, why don't you ever wear that to school?!" And I'm looking at myself and I'm thinking, this is so stupid! Of course I don't wear it to school! That's why it's been at the back of my drawer since I bought it. I would never wear this to school cuz it's not *tznius*. And then it hits me — *omg*! That's the most hypocritical thing I ever heard. You won't wear it to *school,* but wearing it in general is okay?! We said in our last meeting that sometimes there is no such thing as baby steps in *tznius*. You can't start something and not go through with the *kabbalah*. And so, with those noble, sacrificing thoughts, I took off the shirt and put on a plain white tee-shirt and zip up. Go me. But don't celebrate just yet — cuz even though I triumphed over my *yetzer hara* last night, I know what happens every morning when I get dressed. It's hard, and it will always be hard to keep putting up a good fight regardless of whether you win or lose. Sometimes I'm strong enough, sometimes I'm not, but I'm going to keep fighting.

● ● ●

♡ Avigail

It's funny. There are specific stores where *everything* they sell promotes the exact opposite of Torah. I try not to think about what I'm broadcasting (and the price), because I know there is something wrong. But, it's what's cool, and I, along with everyone else, wear it.

It's really hard. Everyone wants to be accepted, and a lot of times that means compromising. Compromising beliefs, such as *tznius*, a certain standard of kashrus maybe, sometimes Shabbos.

How are we supposed to "just say no?" That's really hard.

☆ Chavi

I just got back from a two hour trip to _____. It's a *frum* store that sells dresses and stuff. My mom took me, and the first thing I think when I walk in the door is: "Oh man, here comes my claustrophobia." The fitting rooms were two by four with just enough elbow room to knock down the neighboring fitting room if you hit it at the right angle. I tried on a million dresses, and it's hard when a saleslady tells you that it's okay if your knees are showing, cuz you'll wear black tights. So I left with three dresses. Also, I wasn't with anybody who really knew what I wanted in terms of appropriateness.

There was a sweater dress that I really loved (and that says a lot cuz I hate dresses) but it was so above the knee — really cute though — and the saleslady was trying to make it seem longer, but it didn't work. I asked her if there's anything I can do, like let down a hem or something, and she was like, "Yeah, become less *frum*."

 Rachel

I actually like *tznius* — at least the concept and how I try to dress. I love that it really gives Jewish women more respect from men, and they're not just viewed as pieces of meat. Obviously, I'm human, and I like guy attention just as much as any other girl my age, and I want to look good when boys will be around and act in a certain way around them. But I mean, it's so obvious that at this age, they are all mostly thinking about how you look, and it makes sense to cover up to a certain degree.

Shevi

Some aspects of *tznius* aren't so hard for me. It doesn't really bother me that I can't wear pants, or that I have to cover my elbows and my collarbone. I barely even think about it in the morning when I'm getting dressed. My struggle in the morning and throughout the day, is more to cover my knees — especially when I'm sitting.

I guess one day *that* won't be my main struggle, and I'll have a new one. Because with *tznius* (like everything else Jewish) you never stop or get perfect at something, you just have to keep working.

Ellie

If *tznius* has to do with topics of conversation, what you listen to, what you say, etc., it kinda means that it's gonna have to do with who you choose as friends, which is a little scary.

Sarah

Just wanna talk a second about my little shopping trip with Rachel. Honestly, I don't know why our whole *tznius* group doesn't go on a field trip to the mall together, but okay.

Basically I had a *blast*. I think it was the first time that I've actually enjoyed shopping since I started working on *tznius*. Before that trip, I was always afraid to go cuz I knew how hard it would be. But here, I had her for support and encouragement not to get anything not *tznius*. And, for the first time, I found myself completely focused on the *tznius* clothing — I completely tuned out everything else. For the first time I didn't feel the need to look at all the other stuff and drool over what I *couldn't* get.

So thanks, Rachel, cuz that was pretty cool.

DECEMBER

Tznius FAQ's

THE THIRD MEETING

I started the meeting by reading a letter that had been placed in my box in the teachers' room during the past week. It was a powerful letter, sincere and well-written, and I thought they would want to hear it. Here it is, verbatim:

Dear Mrs. Goldin,

So one time, towards the end of ninth grade, I was at the beach with a friend. Though we were dropped off fully clothed, we had secretly brought miniskirts and tank tops to put over our bathing suits. Quickly changing in the nearest bathroom, we stepped back onto the beach nervous and excited, the adrenaline kicking in and the rush of rebellion clearly getting to our heads.

No one had ever really explained to us the meaning of tznius, the beauty of tznius, or the positive outcomes/repercussions tznius could have. Therefore, we had both felt caged and embarrassed in front of the rest of the world. We were simply sick of looking different all the time! Why did those other girls get to walk around comfortably in bathing suits, while we had to be uncomfortable in soaking wet and heavy clothing?

Now, at this beach, we had been liberated. We strutted along the water's edge looking/feeling "hot" and way too overconfident. We even went so far as to think everyone (namely, boys) was looking at us and us alone. For a short time we were on top of the world. No one was looking at us strangely; we were just like everyone else. We could do whatever we wanted and it wouldn't matter because no one cared, no one looked or stared — we were finally free!

However, the way we were dressed, we were also barely able to look at each other for more than five seconds, and when we did look we'd flush bright red very quickly. Ignoring our guilty consciences, we continued our long afternoon at the beach: tanning, relaxing, and truly feeling like we fit.

This was one of the worst mistakes I've ever made, and one of the worst days I've ever had. Why did we feel good? Because we looked like everyone else. Why was no one staring at us? Because we looked like everyone else. And why were we absolutely invisible to everyone? Because we looked just like everyone else! There was absolutely no kedushah, no separation that made us special to the outside world. Of course, we knew who we were on the inside (and thought that was enough), but by no means did it reflect what we looked like on the outside. Instead of being raised (in social status) to their level, we were shoved down to their level in so many ways. Originally a giddy teenager's plan, looking like everyone else has now become pitiful to me, something I am ashamed of ever having wanted.

As Jewish girls, it is a responsibility and sometimes a hassle to stay covered up like we do, but also, more so, it is a privilege. We stay separate and sanctified like the precious jewels we are. We are noticed and respected and we must believe that even if it doesn't always visibly show. We are not ever disregarded as just one of the crowd; we are exceptional and unique. Our presence in this world is not taken for granted by those around us, unless we take it for granted ourselves.

I don't know if that day was a test I failed or a learning experience I had to go through, but either way I took a lot out of it. It's been a while since that day, but the lessons I have learned will stay with me for a long time, if not forever.

This is just something to maybe discuss at the after-school tznius thing *you run — just an experience shared from one kid to another. I'm not in your program but I think it's amazing. Hopefully through this, kids will realize the values of tznius without having to experience the stupid mistakes.*

Thanks,
A Kid

The girls appreciated the letter as much as I did, and I was glad because it was at this meeting that we were going to begin the hard part.

Until now we had been discussing *tznius* in a very vague way. We spoke about *kedushah*, sensitivities, "looks"...but we never got into specifics. Halachic requirements for clothing? Never touched it.

First we spoke about the fact that girls naturally put a tremendous amount of emphasis on their appearance (do you have any idea how early one needs to wake up in order to perfect that just-rolled-out-of-bed casual look?), but this becomes a problem when we forget that there is a person behind the outfit. No matter what the style, a person's outfit should never be so loud as to outshine themselves. So why not wear matching robes, or have some sort of a national uniform if we care to de-emphasize the external so much? Answer: we want to de-emphasize the external, not negate it. We, as people, are more than how we dress, but I don't believe Hashem just wants us to bury our personal taste and grab the shapeless black dress everyday. Our outside should complement our inside, not overshadow it. It's the side dish, not the main course (there's the weirdest *mashal* I've ever heard, right there).

And with that we began the *halachos*. We spoke about the three main areas in *tznius*: not showing what shouldn't be shown; not wearing anything which could give off a look that would clearly fall under *chukas hagoyim*; and not wearing anything that is provocative in any way. I tried to be very specific, and there were a lot of examples shown and spoken about.

It was a lot to take in all at once, and we spent time talking about how the details and specifics of certain looks are not necessarily about the clothing themselves, the point is more about the specific direction one chooses to face: am I heading toward *kedushah* right now, or not? The point is not to be a paradigm of *tznius*, though that would be nice, the point is to constantly work on ourselves to meet our evolving sensitivities to the issues.

It was a long meeting, and a heavy one. I knew that I had brought up a lot that was new to these girls and discussed clothing in a way that was much more nitpicky than they were used to. I tried to end off with the thought that it's not that Hashem wants so impossibly much from us, it's that He wants so much *for* us: lives of *kedushah*, real relationships based on a deep sense of who we are as people, and the full development of our *neshamos*.

I wasn't sure that they weren't too overwhelmed at the time to hear it, but I was confident that if they found the strength to keep at it, the benefits would reveal themselves with time.

• • •

♡ Avigail

Today is my birthday. That makes me sixteen. Out of those sixteen years, about five of them have been spent fighting with my parents about my clothes. It's been constant, bitter, and usually ends in (my) tears. My parents so badly want me to be the daughter they envisioned, probably since before I was born. But I'm not. I'm the rebel, the one they get embarrassed of in front of their friends. I know their disappointment, they make it so clear.

My sister makes up for it, to a degree. She's a good Bais Yaakov girl, *tznius* and respectful.

Why am I writing all this? Because I realize that this is exactly what turned me off: my parents. They hyperfocus the entire Judaism on this, on clothing. We always argue about the way I dress.

My mom would literally bring her measuring tape to every store. Each skirt had to measure up so that no matter what I'd be doing — sitting, standing, doing cartwheels, my knees would be covered. And then my father would double-check it when we got home. It wasn't normal.

I was always excited when I outgrew a skirt a little bit. I would pull it down in front of my parents, then pull it back up when I left the house. I always felt prettier, more popular in a shorter skirt, even though I know that's stupid. I kinda felt a little bit guilty, but that feeling was way too weak compared to the high feeling of looking good and getting away with something.

Sooner or later though, my mother would take away the skirt. Once I came home from somewhere and found six skirts gone — that was a *huge* fight.

So, my parents are really why I hate *tznius* so much. I never appreciated the beauty or depth of the laws. To me, it was just another set of rules my parents had for me. Now, for the first time, I'm thinking about these things in such a different way.

So here you go. I'm giving you my journal this time along with something else. I got this skirt for Sukkos two years ago. It hits right in the middle of the knee. Of course, at home it's always magically lower. But I know it isn't right and I decided it was time to do something about it.

And here's the worst part of the whole thing. When I told my parents that I thought it had gotten too short for me, their reaction was a couple of minutes of silence, and then a whole tirade of how of course it was too short and I should never wear it again. As if what I said was just a bunch of empty words, and I wasn't actually going to do something about it.

I was sad...disappointed. After all these years, I'm finally doing what they want, and...nothing. It made me want to take the skirt back, honestly. But then I thought, Who am I doing this for really? Me? Or them? Me. For me and G-d — and that's all that matters.

So here's the skirt. I know you have no idea what to do with it. Throw it out for all I care. Make it into a quilt, rip it up and use it as rags, I just don't want it. This is the first time I'm ever doing something like this, and I just want you to know that it's because of this group.

☆ Chavi

I think every day is getting easier and harder at the same time. It's easier because every day that I think I'm dressed better, I get more into it and less uncomfortable. There are things in my closet that I would *never* wear anymore. So why are they still there?

Well, here's the hard part — I can't get rid of them. It's not that I secretly want to wear them anymore, because I don't. My family thinks I'm doing all this stuff and changing because of this group, like I'm being brainwashed or something, and I think if I actually threw out clothes or something, they would "comment," to put it nicely. So keeping the clothes there actually makes this whole thing easier, despite the temptation to wear them.

And there's something else...(Okay, this is going to be a really awkward *mashal*, but stick with me...) It's like a cute puppy that you buy, and then it gets a little bigger and older. And then it hits a size that you really like, and you just don't want it to get any bigger — even though you know it has to — because you just love it the way it looks at that point. Sometimes, I feel like that puppy. Like a cute, adorable puppy that you don't want to grow, because you just love it at the size it is. So I improve a little here, and grow a little there, and I'm okay with that, but I don't want to lose completely who I am now. I guess I mean I'm just taking it really slow for now.

❀ Rachel

What I definitely need to work on is my behavior around guys. I stopped having guy friends a long time ago, but before that I had a ton. I remember that I purposely stood a certain way and was just a totally different person around them. Does any girl *not* put down their friends when trying to make conversation with a boy? I feel like all girls do it to make themselves look better, or even just to make conversation. Anyway, that's not my scene anymore, but I still notice

I get a little that way when there happen to be guys around.

Shevi

I happen to think that low-cut shirts look really nice. I don't mean tanktops, because I really think those look trashy, but I like dresses and some tops that are just pretty and look nice with a lower neck.

A couple of summers ago I went to camp. Low-cut tops were really in then, and I started wearing my shirts way lower then I would've normally. I had the BEST counselor in the world and she really influenced me to throw out a lot of the shirts, so that by the end of the summer I was really covering my collarbone everyday.

I know that may sound funny, that such a minor thing was hard, but that's just the way it was for me. Then. Now I'm past it. I'm not even sure what made me think about that now.

Ellie

I don't get why guys don't have to put up with more of this. I mean, yeah, it would be weird if they had to wear *sheitels* and skirts... but you know what I mean. Why does it all have to fall on the girls?! Also, why can men sing in front of women, but not the opposite? And yeah, when a guy gets all *shtarked* out in Israel he sometimes comes home as an "Oreo" — black hat, white shirt, black pants, and he looks all *frum* and it's a "level thing." But if he doesn't dress like that i.e. — colored shirts, or even shorts, though it isn't maybe considered as nice, it isn't halachically wrong, either. Girls have SO many more restrictions! It's crazy! Obviously, it's because we have more control in this area, no? I guess we really are the ones calling the shots. If not, then I really don't get it.

Sarah

Okay, classes are super boring, it's almost midterms, and I'm just trying to hang in there until midwinter vacation. The only high point of the day is hanging out after school with friends.

And it's making me a little nervous.

For some reason it's been weirdly warm for this time of year, and none of my friends wear tights, obviously, but I don't know, I still am.

I don't want them to think I'm a freak or that this group is totally changing me. I hate it when kids get this holier-than-thou attitude. I don't want to be like that.

• • •

 Avigail

I just realized how many decisions we make regarding *tznius* everyday. And how we have to use our common sense even when it seems like it's obvious what's right.

Shopping is the biggest pain in the neck. Last week I went looking for Shabbos clothes. I tried on two dresses. One of them covered my knees, elbows, and everything, but it was made out of a certain clingy material. I happened to really like it but I got the other one. The only thing is that you told us that *tznius* also means beautiful, and when I put on the other dress (the *tznius* one) I feel ugly. There's something about that awful length that doesn't make me feel pretty. Whatever — it's just hard to convince yourself that you look beautiful in G-d's eyes when you don't look beautiful in your own.

Was that really immature?

☆ Chavi

So, last night we all met and we talked about a bunch of things but mainly the *halachos* of *tznius*. K — I'm not getting it. The skirt past the knees makes sense to me, but I honestly don't get the whole sleeves thing. How is the elbow provocative? I just don't get it. Also, the whole thing you were saying about certain types of styles and shirts and things like that — honestly, I think that's a huge step. I went home last night and felt really stupid about myself. I just don't think I'm ready for all these major steps. But if I'm not careful with *tznius,* does that mean that any good things I do don't count? I don't know, sometimes I feel that my *tefillos* aren't getting through because I don't dress the right way, or that that's why my teachers don't respect me. I feel like teachers point me out in their minds thinking "Well, she used to wear..." or stuff like that. Why do I always feel like people are staring at me?

I know that it's all my fault. Sometimes I feel in my heart that if I truly tried to change I'd fail and feel worse. Don't get me wrong, it's not like I'm not open to change. I want to hear all these things about *tznius*. Maybe I just need to focus more. Yeah, maybe that's it.

So it feels kinda good to vent and write everything that's on my mind. I don't wanna be a bad person, and obviously I'm not saying I am, but these meetings make me feel like *tznius* is the only thing that matters.

✾ Rachel

Ever since I started going through my clothing to give things away, my friends keep asking me for my hand-me-downs. I feel like it's wrong to give them clothing that *I* won't wear — like I'm hurting them.

Shevi

K, so there's something I've been realizing. After each time we meet I get all inspired and have all these ideas of what I wanna do, but then I just forget about it the next day. So this time I really wanna do something about it. So now it's time to say good-bye to my really short jean skirt. I'm thinking about cutting it up, because if I don't I'm still gonna wear it.

Okay, I'm really gonna cut it. Uch, I keep changing my mind and now I don't want to.

K now I'm really gonna cut it. I'll let you know how it goes.

AHHH!! I just went on a rampage and cut three skirts! I think I'm getting a little carried away. It kinda feels like giving a *korban* — I know that sounds weird, but I actually mean it.

I know this is really random, but sometimes I wish my friends would tell me when I'm wearing something not *tznius* because like, we're all working on something or the other. If I'm with my friends and not wearing something good I'd want them to tell me.

Ellie

This week we learned all the *halachos* of *tznius*. Yeah, that was a little crazy. So my question is this: If these things are really *assur*, then how come so, so many people disregard these laws? I end up feeling like everything that I've been told is okay, is not.

I really do understand what you were talking about with *chukas hagoyim*. Recently I got a boy's shirt from American Eagle. I thought it was cute and wore it to school. Last Shabbos, I went on a camp Shabbaton and I wore that shirt Saturday night, but this time I felt like a total dork who was trying to be cool. How could it be that when I wore that shirt the week before I felt so comfortable, but when I wore it this week I felt so out of place and a little un-*tznius*?

I know I keep complaining, "What does G-d want from us already?" — but I also know that it's not what He wants *from* us, its what He wants *for* us.

Sometimes I feel like it's not fair for all the people who aren't learning this stuff.

 # Sarah

K so basically after tonight's meeting I literally feel like garbage. I can not begin to tell you how uncomfortable I was hearing about how against halachah I dress...I *am*.

And I KNOW I'm not half as bad as a lot of kids I know.

So why do I feel like the world's worst Jew?

It just feels really frustrating to be trying so hard and then to hear the things we talked about, and realize that it doesn't really matter because I'm doomed anyway: *chukas hagoyim*, *arayos*, knees, collarbone, elbow, tightness — like, seriously already!

One second you're telling us that wherever we are is fine, as long as we're headed in the right direction — and the next it's like oh, and by the way you're all transgressing like 3000 *issurim d'Oraysa*. Like, oh gee, thanks. Totally not making me feel bad at all. NOT!

You know that feeling of being at the bottom of a long staircase that you need to go up and you are just so tired, and you're looking up at the staircase thinking, "Whoa!"

So right now, that's how *tznius* is for me. Every time I climb a stair I see 8 million more steps ahead of me, tons of other stuff I still stink at, so many more areas and aspects of *tznius* I've never even heard of and I'm just so *tired* of climbing the stupid staircase to *kedushah*. I mean, isn't there an elevator or something?!

But no. I know what's waiting for me at the top of the steps — *s'char*, *kedushah*, awesomeness, and I'm determined to keep climbing no matter how tired I get. Slowly, slowly I will reach the top.

It would help though, if I got less reminders of how much further/ higher I need to climb and more reminders of how many steps of the staircase I've already covered.

Tznius is like a game of chutes and ladders. Keep trying to get to the ladders, and avoid the chutes at all costs. You definitely don't wanna go backwards. It's going UP, it's a raise in spirituality, it's EL-EVATING.

So why it's bringing me down so much I couldn't tell you for sure.

(K, actually, I just realized that was really obnoxious. I know I signed up for this thing and I really do get these concepts, but I'm *not* ready to do anything about it.)

• • •

♥ Avigail

Tznius should not be about the rules. The inches, colors, the blending into the walls. *Tznius* is about accepting yourself as a whole, loving yourself, and looking beautiful.

It's when you look at someone else and say, "Wow. She's living such a *real* life." It sounds cheesy but it's like her soul is shining through. It's because she loves and respects Hashem so much that it turns her into that kind of person. That's what *tznius* means to me.

☆ Chavi

Yeah, so maybe that last entry was kind of dramatic. But at least I got to vent a little bit. So now that my feelings are out there, I can relax. I don't think all the *halachos* should have been sprung so hard on us at one time like that. I think it would have been easier, for me at least, to learn a new halachah each time and work on it individually. I feel it would have been more gradual that way, more step by step, more manageable.

Rachel

What do I do when I see someone who I consider *frum* and amazing, and she's not keeping the highest standards of *tznius*? It happens all the time, and I feel like it makes me second-guess myself. I mean, I know why I dress the way I do, and I won't stop just because everyone else doesn't necessarily hold of that level. Does it say anything about a person if they don't keep things that are not actually halachah but are more under the spirit of the law? I find myself classifying people or making assumptions about them based on whether or not they're dressed up to my standards. Is this wrong? I know it's not so good of me, but I find myself doing it anyway. I mean, how else do you get first impressions? Obviously, the person knows you'll see the way she's dressed and make some sort of assumption based on it. Clearly, she's comfortable with what she's wearing. Does this entry make any sense even?

Shevi

We have two TVs at home. I never really thought that there was a problem with watching TV — it's relaxing, entertaining, and sometimes interesting. But lately I've been thinking a lot about it. First of all, TV is a *huge* waste of time. Not only that, but I realize that everything the Torah tells us *not* to do ends up being played out there on the TV screen! The TV shows that the less you wear the more beautiful you look! I really think it would be 100 times easier to dress *tznius* without a TV. I know these people are not our role models in life, but in terms of beauty...well, I'm just saying that I think it would be way easier to develop a sense of beauty without all this trash being programmed into us from the time we're babies.

♪ Ellie

I have cousins that aren't so close to our family, but visit a lot. They usually show up to my house in really un-*tznius* clothing. I'm not talking tight stuff — I mean jeans, or short shorts and tee-shirts. When I was younger I was really self-conscious wearing skirts around them and stuff, because I felt like a nerd. I'd always ask my mom if I could just stay in my pajamas when they came, because at least I'd still be in sweatpants and wouldn't be embarrassed. So this morning I was hanging around my house and playing with my little brother [still in my pajamas] for a while and kinda lost track of time, and then I heard my cousin's car pull up — I didn't think they were coming for another hour! So I ran upstairs really fast and changed into a *tzanua* outfit, tights and all, before they came in. We ate pizza with them, they bugged me about taking more college credits, about going to some modern seminary they all went to that I've never even heard of, discussed their older sister (in Yale)'s nose ring, etc. until they left. And the whole time I knew that as much as they were bugging me about it, making random comments and everything, I was SO happy dressed the way I was dressed, and talking the way I was talking. Instead of being embarrassed in front of them, I was kinda embarrassed *for* them (which may be a whole nother issue, I don't know).

 Sarah

Right, okay, ready for a long one — because I have a LOT to say.

Cleveland, Cleveland, Cleveland. Home of the frequent snow storms, Cleveland Indians, and the biggest lesson in *tznius* I've had. Cleveland is the kind of place you go to visit relatives. It's not the kind of place you'd normally go on vacation. But it's still pretty intimidating for a "modern" kid like me. My cousin's wedding took place on Thursday night, so my family flew in on Wednesday to stay for the whole weekend. I did *not* want to go. When my cousin got engaged I said, "*Mazal tov!* I'm not going to Cleveland for the wedding." When we found out that I had off from school that Friday, I said, "That's awesome — but I'm still not going to the wedding." But I did and now I'm here. Its *motza'ei Shabbos* now and I have *tons* to write about. But let me first explain what I said before — k, I don't know if it was the *biggest tznius* lesson I have ever had, but this Shabbos was definitely an eye-opener for me. But before we talk about Shabbos, let's go back to Wednesday at the airport.

The cool thing about airports is that you can spot a Jew from a mile away. My brother says it's like this: when you're wearing a yarmulke, or a skirt or *sheitel*, or anything that makes you look obviously Jewish, all Jews will either look at you or look away from you. If they are fellow *frum* Jews, also wearing yarmulkes and skirts, etc., they're looking for you like you're looking for them — everyone is always searching for Jews for minyanim or just to feel like they are not the only Jew in the world. And if they're not religious Jews, their eyes are just as drawn to you because they resent your observance, or maybe they even long for it. Either way, they are looking at you and realizing that they don't look like the *frum* Jew you do, so they look away quickly. But not quickly enough.

I noticed this in the airport with a few Jews that I saw and their individually strange reactions to seeing me with my skirt and tights, my mother with her *sheitel*, and my dad and brother with their yarmulkes, strolling through the airport. They looked at us for a split second too long, and then walked past us and everything we represented to them — on with their lives. So there was a very religious man and his son sitting behind us on the plane, the *Tatty* with his long white beard and the son with his curly long *payos*, talking to each other in Yiddish. I found myself glancing at them self-consciously every five-seconds — kinda uncomfortable about them — almost embarrassed of them, and I realized how those other Jews at the airport must feel. They either look at you, or look away from you, because they are either proud of you (and themselves), or they are embarrassed of you because they are embarrassed of themselves and embarrassed to be Jewish. I know it sounds sad and all that, but I kinda understand it. No one wants to stick out like a soar thumb. We want to blend in: *just blend in.*

Why, though? Why did I feel embarrassed of the guy sitting behind me on the plane? Why did I feel embarrassed of the way I was dressed in the short skirt and tight shirt I was wearing that day? Why can't I just walk around the airport and be proud to be Jewish and look Jewish — I'm never going to see these people again in my life anyway.

And then I got to Cleveland. I walk into my cousin's house and was immediately engulfed and overwhelmed by the number of Bais Yaakov uniforms and black hats and beards that greeted me. My family is pretty big and it just seemed like I had suddenly walked into someone else's *yeshivish* family by mistake. I was determined to hate my cousins because obviously they were going to feel like they were "too good for me." I just wanted to go home. Now that I'm writing this, I realize that if at least four or five of my cousins would have been dressed like me, I wouldn't have had such a bad attitude towards the whole thing to begin with. So it all came back to the way we were dressed. And then I realized that it was not that *their* way of dressing made me feel that they felt superior — it was *my* way of dressing that made me feel like they felt superior. Stay with me here. I cannot tell you how hard it was to have spent the last couple of months feeling like I was changing and improving in my *tznius,* and then come to Cleveland and feel like my entire family was judging me for wearing Uggs and a jean skirt.

And now I realize that it wasn't that they were judging me. It's that I was judging myself. I suddenly felt stupid and underdressed and, regardless of what I wore the entire weekend, I always felt like everyone was looking at me, their modern, quiet (me? quiet!) cousin. And to them, obviously, modern is synonymous with "not *frum.*"

I remember always making fun of very *frum* kids and putting them down. Like, we would say that they may be dressed *tznius,* but they're always speaking *lashon hara.* Or they spend so much time *davening,* but it's all just a show...and other really mature things like that. But people like my cousins keep proving me wrong. They were all like...stalking me a whole weekend — making sure I sat with them, had who to hang out with and all that...always being super nice. At first it really drove me crazy, I thought it was totally obnoxious — like, hello, don't make it so obvious that I'm your *kiruv/chesed* case! Just leave me alone already! But now I see it differently.

They may still wear clothes that I could never imagine myself wearing. They may go to a totally different type of school than I go to, and not understand my *nisyonos* in the world I live in. They may even speak a totally different language than I do. But I know that they're sincere, that they're *not* fake, and they are *not* judging me. If anything, I was judging them.

So what's the big *tznius* lesson I learned in Cleveland? That what you keep saying about where we are in *tznius* is totally true. As long as we are headed to *kedushah*, it's okay not to dress one hundred percent perfectly right away. We are all *bnos Yisrael*, and we are all struggling. I guess in a way, I'm kind of jealous of my cousins. Watching them over Shabbos, they seemed so happy and careless. They just seem to be chilled, and none of them have these major *tznius* battles. Yeah, they may get into trouble for not buttoning the top button in school, or whatever, but the truth is, they don't struggle with the issues I have, they really don't. But I learned that that doesn't matter. I'm sure they each have their individual fights, and we come from different places, different communities, different lifestyles. And it does sting when we all get together, and they seem to have so much in common and I'm just kind of randomly thrown in there. But as long as we're headed in the same direction, nothing else really matters. If I don't want them to judge me, then I can't judge them. It's not the differences that make us judge, really, it's the lack of connection. And in truth, we're all on the same team.

● ● ●

♥ Avigail

There are times when I really wish you hadn't asked me to be part of this thing. Will I ever be able to always choose *not* to wear something just because it's wrong, and not because my parents tell me to, or because I don't want to get in trouble at school? When does this get easier?

☆ Chavi

I know it sounds like all I've been doing is crying about how hard it is for me to change and how overwhelmed I am and all that...but I *have* been changing this whole time. I did let go of a lot of clothes that I was attached to, and I end up wearing the same two skirts all the time, but I really don't care. I'll buy more clothes when I get the chance. I'm also working on *tznius* in speech and actions. Okay, that's a lie really, I'm not focusing on my actions so much. I'm trying SO hard not to use bad language, though. It's really hard. I find myself thinking the words, and then they just slip out. I've picked up these words from here and there, and it's just so easy to get used to them. The problem is that some of these words are so strong, there's this kind of relief that comes with saying them, and you just can't get that feeling from using a different word.

So here's what works for me a lot of times: When I'm talking to a friend, I pretend that I'm talking to a teacher. I would *never* say certain things in front of a teacher, the words would never just slip out without me noticing. So I guess I know from experience that it *is* possible to hold myself back. It's not a perfect plan, but it's been working for me a lot of the time.

Rachel

My friend just got back from visiting her sister in Israel and told me something so inspiring. So everyone knows that most seminary girls have this huge fear of gaining weight, right? So her sister was one of those girls, and from the beginning she organized this whole exercise class for her and a group of friends. So the class ended recently, and all of her friends signed up at a co-ed gym near their school. Some cover up, some don't, but they all go. She decided for herself, that even though the exercising meant so much to her, she wouldn't go to the mixed gym. That kind of strength inspires me so much. *That* is the courage to stand apart.

Shevi

It's funny how I find myself getting really excited whenever *tznius* comes up in class. Like today a teacher was saying all these great things about how women have a natural tendency to want to be focused inward, and cover their bodies, and about what beauty really means and all that, and in my head I was like, yeah, yeah, I know this stuff already...

Ellie

You have no idea how crazy hard I find it to write about this stuff. I don't understand, I'm really good at spewing most of the time, and this is an actual topic that comes up (or should come up) 24/7 and I can never think of anything to write.

Actually, I just filled up four lines saying I don't have anything to fill the lines with. Cool.

I like my crazy color socks. I like walking around in stores wearing dumb hats and huge glasses. There it is — I'm weird, what else is new. Of course, I see the value in not doing awkward things in public so everybody doesn't look at you, and to act as a *bas melech* and all that, but what if that makes me not...me? I'm still convinced no one's really looking at me, and no one cares — besides for my mother — how crazy I act in these places. So yeah. Now I feel like an idiot for writing all of this, because everyone's journals are all deep and stuff and I still don't get why Hashem cares about any of this type of stuff.

Was that really bad to write?

I'm reading this whole spew and realizing it's exactly that — spewage. Sorry, it just came out. I know He cares because we're supposed to be *kadosh* — different and special.

But some things are just *fun*, you know? Like, don't chew gum like a cow or blow bubbles like a valley girl, don't fall down laughing on the floor in middle of the mall, don't order up the whole restaurant and burp loudly afterwards, yeah, obviously. But where is the line between these things and things that are just innocent and fun?

There are some communities where *everything* is not allowed, where even the smallest things are considered inappropriate, and I want to understand their line of thinking. You can see the *kedushah* that they have, and it's really cool, but I still have a hard time getting it. If the tiniest thing becomes an issue, isn't that ridiculously overbearing? I just don't get how they don't feel suffocated.

 # Sarah

I was with a group of kids over Shabbos, and one of them I had just met. She's really nice and cute and funny, a little the crazy type. But I don't know, there was something about her... She's a really big talker, I guess you could say, but beside for just enjoying to talk and talk and talk, she has this way of carrying herself that just comes off wrong. She's very, *very* laid back, and usually that's not a bad thing, but I just feel like there's something refined and modest about keeping your mouth shut occasionally. She kind of bounces and bobs across a room, it definitely attracts people's attention. She just kind of waltzed into my friend's house like she owned the place, and just sort of kicked off her shoes, threw off her coat, and immediately started babbling away about something. And I thought to myself, even with her totally 100% kosher clothing, she still comes across as less *tznius* than me. At least, if you know what *tznius* really means.

To people who think *tznius* is only clothing, she's just the really outgoing type, and there's nothing wrong with that. And there isn't. Except when there is.

JANUARY

Thinking Out Loud

THE FOURTH
MEETING

When the girls returned to school from midwinter vacation, I gave them a chance to drop out of the project. This project had started as a totally voluntary undertaking, and even though I had originally asked them to commit for the whole year, I was nervous about going ahead when I felt that they were not all ready to continue the way I had envisioned. I wanted them to start thinking about how they could work on *tznius* in practical terms, as opposed to just recording their observations but not necessarily doing anything concrete. To be honest, I probably wouldn't have pushed them if not for the fact that I wanted their journals to include their experiences as they began to change, and I felt it was only fair to allow the kids who didn't want to focus in that way an escape. Four kids did choose to leave the group, though one continued to write in her journal until the end of the year.

The fourth time we met it was a smaller group of girls, and they were all committed and willing to push themselves. All ten of the original kids are special, but now the group was energized in a way they hadn't been before. We didn't discuss any one topic at the meeting, I just read out some of their journal entries, and let them decide which issues to talk about.

• • •

♡ Avigail

You told me today we're "taking it into the next level," and that I'm either in or out — but I really don't know! A lot of times I feel that I don't know what *tznius* requires, what it entails. It's so easy to write about but so hard to do.

I want to know, Is *tznius* a compromise on fun and normal teen-age behavior? Does being a complete *tzanua* mean I can never put on more than a little bit of makeup, cuz then I'm giving off an overly whatever message?

I really don't know... I feel like I'm two different people. One is the *tznius* one and the other is not. I want to merge them but I can't. I can't help it, sometimes I just go completely insane and get so mad at my parents and mad at G-d for demanding so much, and I let it out by rebelling. And then there are those days where I feel so spiritual and connected — and now you're just going to think I'm nuts.

But you should know that those rebellious days are not because I become so overwhelmed with *tznius* that I can't take it. I love *tznius*, I love what it stands for, I love its beauty and everything.

I just know that being *tznius* — really, truly *tznius* — is a huge challenge because...I like attention. Am I normal?

✫ Chavi

I've been pushing this off for way to long — I need to throw away my clothes. I've been ignoring them for a long, long time.

Well, I'm thinking, the sooner the better with this kind of thing. Like volunteering to do a homework project on the earlier date rather than the later one, cuz you know you're going to have to do it anyways. No point in procrastinating so much, wouldn't want to get left back in tenth grade for one stupid project! (SO not worth it.)

Why I've kept my clothes the whole time: (1) I barely have any clothing, so keeping them makes me feel like I have more. (2) JIC scenarios (just in case) — not that I ever want to run into one, but let's say for some reason I really, really need something I gave away? (3) My mother would freak if I threw out all these clothes. Which brings me to (4) What to do with it all?

Yeah, I know, lame excuses, but still...WHATEVER. Bottom line is I want to do it tomorrow when I get home. I'm just scared my mom's going to yell at me for all the money I'm throwing out the window. She knows how to make me feel so guilty.

❀ **Rachel**

Two summers ago, on an amazing summer program, I decided to start wearing tights every day. I was talking to a counselor who happened to give me a good enough reason, so I decided that I should. I came home, and my mother would *not* buy me tights. She couldn't understand the concept of tights in the summer. I had to get my friend to buy my tights for me, and then pay her back with my money. We went to Florida that January, and it was awful. I cried almost the whole time, cuz almost everything turned into a tights fight. Even my grandmother told me I was being stupid and irrational.

Now my family is used to it. As I got older, people started accepting it and seeing it as a good thing. As opposed to when I came back to school right after that summer program and half my friends decided I wasn't cool any more.

My biggest problem is that now I've been in the same place *tznius*-wise for so long, and I know that if I don't want to go down, I have to go up. But do what? I don't know what I would change now.

Shevi

One time when I was in ninth grade, I was *dying* for an Abercrombie zip-up. I thought they were the coolest things ever and everyone had one. Finally, my mom bought me one — these zip-ups weren't cheap. Now it's sitting on the top shelf of my closet — I don't like it at all. I hate having the word ABERCROMBIE written across my front. It just reminds me of what a stupid freshman I was. I think that store should be shut down.

Ellie

So, everyone makes mistakes... Well, most people anyway. The difference is, some people know that what they're doing is wrong as they're doing it, and some people just don't get it.

At the end of elementary school, I had REALLY low self-esteem. Before then, I was a pretty confident kid, but for some reason those couple of years were really hard for me. I didn't like the way I looked and became obsessed with what I ate and when I ate it, and didn't really think about much else. I lost some of my close friends, because they didn't really know how to deal with what I was going through, which just added to the mess. I put on an award-winning show in front of my parents, and if I slipped and acted depressed once or twice, it was because "I was just becoming a teenager" and they let it slide.

The more I let the friendships with my classmates weaken, the more friendly I became with the guys in my community. Because the thing about them was that the more I hung out with them, the more often they would slip in the occasional, "You know, you're pretty" or, "You look good," and as much as I didn't believe them (which of course made them say it more often) it felt good... I figured that it would give me confidence, eventually.

Well, a year later I was in high school, became friends with lots of new girls, and was even a bit skinnier, but besides for that, I was still that same kid. My guy friends were my closest friends, and over time I learned what to do to get those compliments I needed. Outside I looked happy and confident, because I had learned how to put on a show. The truth was, I still hated myself — I hated how I looked, acted, what I said and when I said it, where I went and with who. But I stuck with it all, convincing myself that by living like that I'd get my confidence eventually, and be as happy as I looked. And spiritually? Being the only girl who was *shomer negiah*, who didn't curse as often as she said hi, I was considered the "*frummy*" of my group. So I still assumed I was doing okay.

I continued to let everything be based on my exterior, and the way I perceived myself was based almost entirely on how others claimed to perceive me. I didn't do what *I* wanted to do, I did what my friends told me I wanted to do, and let myself believe that's what I wanted, too. I was in a crowd and place that I thought would help me get to where I wanted to be. Instead, though, I was hating myself more and more for it, and I couldn't find a way out. Finally, I began to understand that if I wanted to be happy, this wasn't the way to do it. So, last minute, I switched my summer plans to a more religious program, and I figured I'd wait to see what happened. The things I learnt there started me on a very different road from the one I was on before. The changes I made and the things I do differently now —

Time out.

1. This is getting SO CHEESY and I really hate that.

2. I don't really know where I'm going with this yet, and it's starting

to turn into some oddly twisted autobiography. But bear with me, alright? Kay thanks.

Time in.

— like the longer sleeves and skirts, collarbone and tightness... Really, it isn't about the technical stuff at all — gradually, those just become the guidelines for something bigger. It took me a pretty long time to realize that *tznius* isn't a dress code. But, it was worth waiting for because now I get to live the way I want to live, according to my own standards. I know I've got things to work out still, and lots to work on — but now I really do love myself. I'm finally happy with the way I look — though superficially I don't look *that* different from the way I did in ninth grade. I like the way I look now because I'm wearing what I'm wearing and doing what I'm doing for the right reasons (most of the time). And when I take a second to think about where I stand as a person, or why I'm doing something, it's because I know they are things that I feel comfortable doing...and what I think/ hope Hashem wants from me, too. I mean, He's really the only One who counts. And besides my own, He is the only opinion that I care about. If He thinks I look prettier in a button-down than a half-sleeve Abercrombie, and so do I, then no one, especially not some boy, could convince me otherwise.

Thank you for listening and enjoy the rest of your evening.

Sarah

Oh man, where do I begin? So you came to me and you said you want to step up this whole thing — want us to share more, write more, and most of all, really work on the mitzvah instead of just thinking about it. And (as you know) I freaked out. Here's why...

First of all, you were giving people the chance to back out. I don't want to end up being the "worst" in the group. I know that sounds stupid, I'm just afraid that everybody on my level is going to back out of this, and I'm going to have the most to work on... Okay, obviously that's garbage and I know it. It happens to be that because of this whole thing, I know that each of us is on her own level, and each of us is working on herself. So know that, regardless of who leaves and who stays, I plan on making sure that I stay aware of this for the rest of the meetings.

Also, I really am afraid to start working on *tznius* in a serious way. Thinking about it is one thing, and even if I'm dressing a *little* differently, that's different from actively saying, this month I'm working on making sure not to wear tight shirts.

Because when you're not *actively* working on something, and you're just *thinking* about acting, it's inevitable that for that entire month you're only going to see the tight shirts in your drawer, and suddenly its like — omgsh, I have no more good shirts! Oh well, guess I'll have to wear this (really cute) tight one until I buy more! I mean come on, stop kidding yourself already.

I don't want to stop kidding myself. I know this isn't how you meant it, but it felt kind of like you were saying — now it's time to get real. No more pretending you're into it but not dressing like it. It sounded like you were saying that if you're even the least bit unsure if you're ready, maybe it's just better to hand in your journal and that's it. Now, I don't give in so easily, ever, and especially not when 99% of me is screaming against it. I *want tznius*. I want it SO badly. But there's that small part of me that doesn't know if I can handle it. It's not that it's too hard, or that it's too soon — I used to think age mattered, but I see that it doesn't.

I guess even if I still kid myself sometimes, and even if I sometimes dress *tznius* and sometimes I don't, I guess it can be a good thing. It means I'm not perfect. It means I still have room to work on myself. And as long as I'm making mistakes, I'll keep working and improving. I think a small part of me will always be afraid to change — either because no one else is doing it and I feel like a loser, or because I just don't feel confident or pretty in those types of clothing. But that fear will make me stronger — it will give me a reason to do just that — wear the clothes no one else will, make a statement, prove myself to myself — because in the end, I'm the one who's judging.

So after all the emotional stress and freaking out (which only goes to show how much I CARE about this), I think I've come to the realization that this is for the best. Even though as far as numbers go, this group won't be changed so drastically, I've already begun to feel a little more pressure to dress right. But it's not a bad kind of pressure — it just reminds me that this is a privilege and a responsibility and if I want it so badly I can totally do it, no matter how old, young, confident, or insecure I am.

So, um , thanks (after all that...lol).

• • •

♡ Avigail

Sometimes I really can't stand my parents. I don't know why they do the things they do. I don't know why they think that force is the answer to everything. I don't know why they feel that by taking away some of my clothing, I'm going to start "appreciating" *tznius* more and start dressing like my mother.

Are they acting like this out of desperation, because they feel they have no choice? It's scary, because the more they act like this, the more they push me away. I've come so far in *tznius* and I don't know why they can't see that.

I wish they would take a parenting class or something.

☆ Chavi

School is getting weird. This one girl came over to me today and asked me if I thought her clothes that day were *tzanua* and stuff. I'm very confused.

When I think about school this year, and school last year, I must come off as a totally different person to the teachers. So which one is me? The hyper, popular one, or the quietish, well-behaved one?

Because I think both are somewhat fake. Maybe the first a little more than the second, but still. I don't like the conversations that go on in my class, because I can never relate to them anymore.

Random: A junior came up to me today and told me that she thinks I'm great. She doesn't even know me. Whatever.

Rachel

I don't know if this comes under *tznius*, but I think I need to work on the way I act. I have this certain air of "knowing I'm cool" which completely disgusts me when I think about it. I can't really describe the feeling, except for saying that sometimes I feel like I think too much of myself and it shows. I don't know how to deal with this, I guess it's *ga'avah*, and it scares me, because it goes against everything I've been working so hard on these past few years.

Like, I think I'm so great because I dress *tznius* and I'm still cool — I don't want to think like this, but how can I stop it?

Shevi

So I went to the mall with a whole bunch of friends and we were having an amazing time, getting all loud and hyper. Then I realized that people were looking at us, and I got really embarrassed and knew we weren't acting *tznius*. I used to just go with the flow and the louder I was, the more fun I was having, but this time...it just felt wrong. Without making a big deal about it, I made sure we toned down and you know what — we had just as good a time.

Sometimes I think (this totally has nothing to do with anything) that people who dress with *tznius* are more approachable. I'm just more comfortable being around people who dress with dignity, like I would sooner go to that type of person if I needed help with anything. It's interesting.

♪ Ellie

I want to be done with school already. I'm tired of going through the process of growing up, I just want to be the person I'm supposed to be. Like, I don't want to have to work on *tznius* anymore, I just want to be a *tzanua*. It's so frustrating.

Lately I'm finding myself very unfocused and I don't know why. Like, I get into these phases when I'm working on my *davening*, *chesed*, *tznius*, and everything is just flying, and then randomly I fall into these ruts where I just feel very little connection to Hashem. I guess that's normal, no?

It's almost midwinter vacation. I wish I was doing something exciting.

Sarah

When you're in the passenger seat of a car, you don't have to focus on the wheel or the road. You can stare out the window and watch the world go by, observing and analyzing and laughing at all the random things moving past you. You can fall asleep, space out, play games, or count license plates like the nerd you are.

But when you're driving, it's different. When you're the one behind the wheel, you can only be focusing on three things: yourself, your vehicle, and your destination. This is no place to be spacing out or falling asleep behind the wheel. You're not at liberty to watch all the people doing their own thing, because then you'll crash — and you'll never reach your destination.

And that's how it is when you're working on *tznius*. When you're in the passenger seat, and you're not really working on it, you can look at other people's actions all you want, and you can compare them and analyze them — you can afford to space out, to "fall asleep." But when you're in the driver's seat with your GPS set to "*tznius*," it's a different ball game. When you make the decision to start working on *tznius*, you need to put all your focus on three things: yourself (and not what everyone else is doing), your vehicle — what you're working on now — and your destination, what you eventually want to become. Because if you look out the window at everyone else and start comparing yourself to them and seeing what they're doing, or if you fall asleep at the wheel and lose sight of what you're working on, you'll crash and never reach your destination.

So you keep your eyes on the road, and when your *bushah* tells you in that little annoying voice, "In .3 miles, make a right turn" or whatever, *listen to it.* Don't suffocate your internal *bushah*, don't brake your GPS or you'll get lost. Just buckle up, take a deep breath, put your key in the ignition, and hit the gas — make the move. Take the step in *tznius* that will propel you forward. And after that, just (be quiet and) *drive.*

• • •

♡ Avigail

So after our last meeting, I just have to say something about that loved/hated addictive website, Facebook.

Ellie put it so well. Girls spend tons of time making themselves look exactly how they want themselves to look, take a million pictures, and then spend hours choosing which ones to post. Then people comment, "Wow, you look so awesome in those pictures," and the kid answers, "Omgsh, I didn't even like that one."

Seriously, who do you think you're kidding?! Everyone knows you spent an hour ironing your hair and putting on the eyeliner just so you could say that!

I hate that whenever friends go out and have a great time it's like it didn't really happen unless everyone else knows about it. Everybody is constantly updated on everybody else's life — even people who you aren't friends with. And then everyone takes apart the pictures:

what everybody looks like, who was with who...let's say I don't want my picture posted online for everyone to talk about?

And that's why that's the end of my facebook. I deactivated my page when I got home last night, and I'm so happy I did.

☆ Chavi

You know, when you first offered me a chance to be a part of this whole thing, I was definitely open to change, but I was still really... wary about the whole thing. Now things are happening so fast that it's hard to keep up with myself.

It started with tights under my short jean skirts, and then it grew to some longer skirts. It continued by trying not to think in a certain way, and it affected how I behaved, and all that. I'm not sure how this all happened, but I'm sure that I don't want it to stop. I just want to make sure that I know what to do next, because I never want to slow down.

At the beginning I used to think, "Why don't people just skip to the most extreme form of *tznius* if that's the best?" Now I know that there's a certain feeling that comes when you go one step at a time, not standing still, but not skipping steps, either. You slowly feel the change in your life. It's really weird because there's this one girl I'm friends with who always says to me, "Stop judging me." I find it so hard to know what to answer back without sounding obnoxious — like, why do you always assume I'm thinking about you?! I think it's just her way of telling me that she can tell that I'm changing and she's not sure what that means about me now, about us.

Whatever. I really don't care what people think — especially about things like how I dress or act.

All I want to know is: Where do I go from here?

Rachel

I think that drawing lines when it comes to *tznius* (and everything else) is extremely important. I think that my lines are pretty subconscious for the most part, and they've just become a part of who I am. Here they are:

My skirts must cover my knees, even when I'm sitting — which sounds a lot easier than it is.

No short shirts, like shrugs or crop shirts — I just find that they look a little trashy. Even the cute ones just end up looking cheap.

Tights — tights I started two years ago, because of a *madrichah* I had. Up until that point I never understood the reason for wearing the see-through kind of tights – the ones that you can still see your legs — it's just another layer to wear in the hot summer, etc. So one day I was talking to this *madrichah* and I randomly asked her what is the point of wearing tights. So she told me that a lot of it is about the person wearing them. There is no denying that when a person is wearing tights on their legs they're aware of it. They are like a constant reminder to the wearer to behave in a more *tznius* way. For me, that was a good enough reason, and I've been wearing them ever since.

Slits — slits I don't wear just because they get too risky with showing more of your leg than you want to. Also, to me it's a now-you-see-it, now-you-don't game, and I just stay away.

I don't wear those spaghetti-strap tops with shirts underneath. It's so obvious that they're meant to be worn without a tee-shirt, and wouldn't that fall under the whole *chukas hagoyim* thing? They look pretty dorky anyway.

I think that words across the front are inappropriate, so I don't wear them.

I think the clearer you are with what you will and won't wear, to a certain extent, the easier *tznius* becomes.

Shevi

I went shopping with my sister and I found a skirt and two tops, so I went to try them on. I tried on a black bubble skirt which looked too small even on the hanger. Obviously it was too short, but I was trying to convince my sister that it was fine by wearing it really low. I don't even know why I was so attached to this skirt, it wasn't even anything special. I went to pay for it, and then I started to think about how this was a test and I shouldn't buy it because I'm working on my skirt lengths and stuff. But the other part of my mind was saying that it looked really cute on me and I really needed another skirt. I was next in line and I thought about everyone else in the group, and how if I bought this skirt it wouldn't help the "cause." I've been working too hard for me to buy this skirt now. I spaced in, put the skirt back, and left the store. Fast.

Ellie

I liked this past session a lot. First of all it's much better with a smaller group. And I love hearing everyone's journal entries, even though I get embarrassed when you're up to mine. The *tefillah* you gave us was awesome.

I stupidly told my sister about these meetings. She laughed and told everyone that I'm part of a "*tznius* club." Pretty embarrassing. My family better not know that this is my journal or I'll die.

Sarah

I hate getting in trouble for *tznius* in school. Who are the teachers to correct us on *tznius* when they barely know us? I've gotten "stopped" for the way I've been dressed, but basically just for friendly reminders, and it's only happened once or twice, which is why what happened today caught me so off guard.

I have this teacher, who I totally and completely LOVE. I'm not a huge fan of her subject, but I barely space out in her class, and I'm actually doing pretty well. My whole grade is obsessed with her. And yet, there is nothing crazy special about her. She doesn't teach in any special or loud way, and outside of class she barely talks, but everyone can tell that she's an incredible person. I promise, she *glows*. Regardless of how little she talks, you end up liking her so much that you just want to be like her. And even without flaunting it, her beauty is so obvious.

So I'm always trying to talk to her to see how she'll respond. Everyday before she leaves I say good day/night/Shabbos. And the whole time I thought she didn't even know who I was outside the classroom. I thought she just figured I was some girl being polite, if she even cared enough to spare me a thought, which I doubt. Doubted. Doubt. (How do you write that?)

Anyways, for the most part, I figured she liked me, but didn't especially notice me. I thought wrong. Unless I'm totally off on my judgment of her (which would be sad after like a whole page of description), she's not the type to randomly correct people on their dress. But now I realize that just because she comes off as quiet it doesn't mean she doesn't notice anything. Let me explain.

Basically, I was walking down the hall at the end of the day and she was coming from the opposite direction, and we just kind of looked at each other awkwardly. And I go, "Have a good night," and she sort of half nods and goes, "Pull up your shirt, Sarah," and I guess I was so not expecting it that I didn't even hear her. "What?" I said, moving closer. She motioned to her own neckline and pulled upward, "It's a little low, pull it up," she repeated. "Oh, ok," I said, pulling up my shirt a little, "Thanks." I smiled, she smiled, and I walked away totally confused.

WHAT?! And I'm thinking, did that just happen? It's just too random. I mean, obviously she cares about *tznius*, but it just makes so little sense to me that out of all of the girls she teaches, most of whom are dressed worse than me, she calls *me* out on a *tznius* thing! I'm not insulted — I'm happy she said something to me, but I'm just confused. I want to think that she only said something to me cuz she likes me and wants the best from me, but at the same time I can't help thinking that she's been watching me and sees a girl that's *so* not *tznius*, that she *had* to say something. I'm so scared to think that. I do not want to believe that after all this work and time and effort I've put into *tznius*, someone will look at me and see that.

Just tell me its cuz she likes me. Please.

• • •

♡ Avigail

My friends that found out about this group think it's really weird. Originally everyone was curious, I really didn't want to tell them exactly what it's about. But eventually it got out that it's *tznius*. So some gave me this sympathetic look, and others rolled their eyes and laughed. I went, "Yeah, I know, it's really weird." Or sometimes if I had enough courage, "It's pretty cool."

Why do kids think that girls who care about religion are nerds?

Now, some friends told me that they think what I'm doing is great, and they respect me for it. Whatever.

☆ Chavi

If you take a strawberry, a perfectly good-tasting, fresh red one, would you automatically jump to judge it and say that something's missing? No. And if you dip that strawberry into chocolate, would it really change? It's not like the chocolate gets in through the pores of the strawberry, totally changing the status of the berry. It's just an added layer, a nice touch to the already fine-flavored fruit. Do you honestly think that the strawberry becomes more spiritual just because it's wearing chocolate? Do you think it's possible to totally change who you are because of the clothing that you wear on the outside? Because sometimes I don't really think that's how it happens. I don't think that the outside can permeate through to your soul. I think there's too much of a gap between both worlds, inside and out. So people choose to focus on whichever they deem more important.

But why can't there be some sort of an exchange in-between — why shouldn't there be? If a girl wears provocative clothes, chances are she'll start acting it, no?

Wait, so if I just established the outside *does* affect the inside, at least negatively, who's to say it can't do so positively? That wearing *tzanua* clothes could eventually lead that girl to act that way. Hmm. It only makes sense that it would work.

You know, people say that I'm getting brainwashed, but the only one who can brainwash is me. So if I decide right now, on my own, that I wanna change, then I can, and that will change the inside Chavi.

It happens to be that I really do like the chocolate.

Rachel

I think that there is a difference between showing interest in dressing in style, and needing to dress totally funky every single day to feel cool. I think that dressing like that, even if you fulfill the requirements of *tznius*, is wrong. Why care about clothing so much? It gets embarrassing, ya know? If you want to, dress cool for yourself, but don't go all-out crazy.

Shevi

VACATION! I was (am) beyond excited...but also a little bit nervous. Whenever people asked me what I'm doing and I say Miami, they go, "You're so lucky." So the truth is...I am very lucky, but I'm also very scared. Miami is like...social scene, and honestly...I hate social scenes. I know everyone is going to be dressed a certain way, and I always end up being the most *frum*-looking one and I know it shouldn't bother me but it really does. Sometimes I feel that it's easier to be *tznius* in a place with cold weather, but the truth is that when I don't give in in Florida it makes me feel really good and accomplished.

♪ Ellie

So if you trust that Hashem is in control of everything, and is the Ultimate Power, and really the One in charge...if you really believe that, then how can we not trust that what He tells us to do is worth it and for our own benefit?! If someone you look up to and trust gives you advice that you don't really think will help or that you don't understand, wouldn't you follow the advice just out of respect for that person? I have, lots of times, and it will happen again and again, because we don't have to understand everything in order for it to be worthwhile or productive. Well, if you believe that...this is G-d we are talking about. He MADE us — He didn't have to but He did — for us. Parents tell us to do realllllly annoying stuff sometimes (a lot of the time) but I hear that when we are older, some of that stuff might pay off. Whether it be with responsibilities or just learning basic social/life skills you can only learn at home. I just turned into my mother for a second, sorry!

G-d asks us to do really annoying things every day, too...but only by doing them can you begin to realize that they're anything but annoying. Constructive. Fulfilling. I have no clue what they are supposed to feel like, because I'm so not there yet — I'm still in the "forcing myself" stage most of the time...but I do know that I'm going to get it eventually, and that already kind of makes it worth it — imagine how more worthwhile it will be, when I actually do get it.

Sarah

I don't have as much to write during vacation as I thought I would. Turns out *tznius* isn't as challenging when you stay home during winter break. I don't have to deal with the whole what-to-wear-to-the-beach thing, or the question of wearing or not wearing long sleeves and socks in Florida and California...but obviously, it is still challenging. Originally, me and a few of my friends organized this whole huge trip to the city. We invited like ten random people, who invited another five random people, and we were planning to go ice-skating and out to eat and shopping. And of course, some of the group ended up being boys. I'm not going to lie, I was more than a bit nervous about this plan.

First of all, some of the people didn't even know each other because it was such a random group, and second, I just wasn't in the mood. Plus, it's like I said before — since I'm home I don't really have that many challenges to face over vacation. It's freezing and boring, so why create problems for myself by meeting up with other girls' guy friends?

So I backed out last minute, saying I wasn't feeling well. I actually wasn't, to tell you the truth. But I knew it was just an excuse. I ended up hanging out all day, and sleeping over by a different girl, and we had a total blast anyway.

FEBRUARY

Peer Pressure Ups and Downs

THE FIFTH MEETING

What comes to mind when I say "*tznius*"?

- Beautiful
- Important
- Respect
- Deep
- Confident
- Low ponytail (?!)

February's topic was peer pressure. There are two sides to peer pressure. The first one is the obvious: people find it hard to change how they dress or act, even if they know that right now it's wrong, because of how other people will perceive those changes. It's very scary not to do something most people around you are doing; for that matter, it's also scary to be doing something that most people are *not* doing. No one — especially not a teenager — wants to stick out of her group.

But the truth is that I wanted to focus on the flip side of peer pressure. I had heard this thought from Mrs. Press in a speech she had given about *tznius,* and it provided a complete paradigm shift for me. I simply had never thought about peer pressure in that way, and I hoped the girls would find it as empowering a thought as I did.

We all tend to think of ourselves as the victims of peer pressure. In our eyes, we are always the little sheep surrounded by wolves. But who are we if not those same wolves?!

Tznius is a unique mitzvah in that most decisions we make are public ones. In that sense, the peer pressure *we create* dictates what is appropriate, or not, to wear. We are setting the standards for our friends.

I wanted these girls to understand the power they had when they chose to be beautiful, cool, and *tznius.* I wanted them to be the ones to set the styles and the standards instead of following them. I tried to get them to realize what teachers know instinctively — that every single girl unconsciously provides a model for other, younger kids.

Teenagers have a hard time admitting this. The girls kept insisting that no one cared what they did, that they couldn't possibly be anyone's role model. I knew they were wrong. This very group, for the continuation of the year, would prove themselves wrong time and again.

We ended off talking about what to do when you find yourself in a situation where you're growing at a faster pace than your friends. It's an extremely delicate problem for high-school girls and one with no good solutions. You can tell a kid to get new friends, but that's a lousy piece of advice, and both of you know it. To make sure you're being a loyal friend, sometimes to people you've grown up with, while continuing to be true to yourself and your own spiritual needs is a tough balance.

• • •

♡ Avigail

It's true — sometimes I'm a loser and a lot of times I really don't project how I am inside, instead I sort of put on this mask to look like...what is it again? Oh yeah — every single other teenage girl.

Why do we always have to look like clones of each other? Like, "Oh look, another American Eagle shirt, let's give her a gold star."

☆ Chavi

Okay, so I have a question: does *kibud av va'eim* override *tznius*? Sometimes (meaning, a lot of the time), I feel like my family puts me in a situation and tries to shove me in their direction. I hate that they split my road in two and force me to choose. It's like I'm getting so much opposition over these little things that I do and I find myself needing support, even though I know what I'm doing is right. I don't want to lose my drive — my ability to separate what's easy from what's right.

Am I going to wear tights in the summer? I think so. I want to be able to do whatever I need to do to be who I want to be. I wish my parents wouldn't be making this hard for me, I never would've thought they would.

❁ Rachel

Tonight I went to the Gap with my mom. I went to the fitting room to try on a bunch of stuff, and toward the middle of the pile of clothes, I tried on a button-down that was really fitted but not necessarily tight. I thought it was okay but I called in my mom to see it, and she said, "I don't know, do you think it looks a little bit tight?" *She* made *me* see the tightness of the shirt, and got me the next size up, which I ended up loving.

This experience actually made me realize how grateful I am that I'm at the point where my mom has the respect for me and my *tznius* that she would tell me when something looks tight. I was so surprised that she was helping me with this. My mom is really great.

Shevi

I was just thinking... I saw pictures on the computer of a girl I know, and she was totally not dressed okay — the pictures were *really* inappropriate. I was good friends with her last year, and we are still friendly this year, but when I saw those pictures it made me look at her differently, and kind of...distance myself a little bit. I feel really badly about it, cuz she is really sweet, but she keeps putting these types of pictures up. She totally sees nothing wrong with it, and it makes me wonder. I can't help staying away.

Ellie

I know these are not supposed to be letters — but, about what you said to me today — I don't really get why you think everyone is looking at me. Sometimes I get the feeling that either you think I am way better than I am, or you think that kids see me as way better than I am. If we have kids in the school (and obviously, we do) who wouldn't be caught dead in anything less then perfectly *tznius*, then why does it make sense for people to be looking at me? I have slits that I haven't gotten around to sewing up, a couple of months ago I was still deciding if I would wear flip-flops this summer, and yeah, when I run out of clothes I wear a shirt that I know that I should not still own. I own red, wear bright yellow when I'm in the mood, and I'm constantly working on not doing ridiculously stupid things in public...and people really know this about me. So why was what I was wearing today so different? I know I shouldn't have worn it, but I hate when you make it sound like I'm on display as a certain standard; I'm really not.

Sarah

I went shopping today for the first time since winter break. And I made a sacrifice that I know for a fact I wouldn't have come even close to making a month or two ago.

I was in H & M (one of the best stores *ever*) and I was trying on some stuff. One of the sweaters I was trying on was ADORABLE — one of those rare types that I felt like I looked pretty good in. But of course, it was a little tight. And by a little, I mean that by your standards probably too tight, but by my usual standards, really flattering. Maybe I was in an especially good mood and I was willing to give up an incredibly cute sweater, or maybe all the stuff about *tznius* seeped into my head a little, but either way, I suddenly looked in the mirror, and I thought, Hmm, it's a little tight. I can do better than this. Let me check if they have the next size up. Of course they didn't. So I did something I definitely would not have done two months ago: I put the shirt back, paid for the rest of my totally *tznius* clothes ☺ and walked out. Kinda cool actually, cuz I felt really good. I wasn't even sad about it.

• • •

 Avigail

This past weekend I went to a different community for a Shabbaton, and I noticed something that really bothered me.

A lot of the advisors weren't dressed okay. I don't know why this bothered me so much. There were definitely kids there that didn't look *tznius* either, but that didn't bother me as much. I don't know,

I guess I was just surprised because I had assumed that people who were willing to give so much of their time to run an amazing Shabbaton like this one, were people who were, I don't know, really *frum*. Now don't get me wrong — I know that not-such-religious people can also do (and *do* do) amazing *chesed*, and I also know a lot of really *frum*-looking people who are not all that great once you get to know them. But, I guess it was an association I had just made that I had expected all these people to just...look holier than they did. I just felt that the way they were dressed took away a little from what they were doing.

✰ Chavi

I had a friend over for Shabbos, and she was asking me all these questions like why am I changing, isn't it hard... She was getting really into it, like she had been thinking about having this conversation for a while. She started by saying that she feels like I stick out from my group. Like she flat out, point blank said, "You stand out because you're the only one dressing like this." Then she was talking a lot about how you can't just change on the outside and all that stuff that I was always saying a couple of months ago...it was weird. And she asked me how I do the whole covering the neckline thing and we just talked. I could tell that she was bothered by the way she dressed — like she wanted to change but she had no drive. We talked about it for a really long time. It turned out she had a lot on her mind and I was just so happy that at least one of my friends (so not that I think badly of my friends *at all*) are thinking about the way they dress. It just seems like they don't care about these things, but they so do. At least, some do.

Rachel

I have this friend who is just so great. I think you can tell a lot about a person based on whether or not she follows the dress code in school even if she doesn't dress that way at home. I think it shows a certain maturity. This friend of mine always covers her legs in school, even though she wouldn't necessarily at home, out of respect for the school and for the kids who do that all the time. It's not at all to be fake or to pretend she is someone she's not, she's just comfortable enough with herself to be able to say, I may not do this all the time, but I'm willing to do it to make *you* more comfortable. So many times, kids have zero respect for other people's standards of religion — like, they say, "If she's gonna be so *frum* about everything, let her just stay home, or find different friends, or hang out someplace else..." No! Why can't we just say, hey, we're all on the same team here, and I like/respect you enough to not do certain things, or to do certain things, for no other reason other than to make you feel comfortable?

You know what I mean?

Shevi

I went to a *vort* recently and all of my classmates and a lot of my teachers were there from elementary school. When I walked in and saw my old group — most of whom went to a different high school — at first I felt like a complete outcast because I was the only one who was dressed to the standard of *tznius* that I was comfortable with. But I forced myself to go say hi to them and be friendly and everything. I kept reminding myself — like, literally talking to myself in my brain — that I do not need other kids' approval for what I wear. We all got along really well and just then an old teacher of mine who everybody loved walked over to say hello, and she gave me the nicest compliment about how I looked. I totally turned tomatoes, but I was really happy she said that.

Also, can I say something else? I HATE when people curse in front of me. I know some kids think I'm a nerd, but it really means a lot to me. I get so upset, and there's nothing to say, besides for which it's after the fact, so why bother saying anything even if I could think of something good to say. I just find it so insensitive. It's like, if you want to do something low and gross in your own life, no problem, but don't make everyone else in the room listen to it. And then, it sort of gives everybody else permission to talk like that too, it just brings down the language level so quickly. I always just stare at the person. Like, yeah, you're really cool.

♪ Ellie

Okay, so I hung up the phone after an *annoying* conversation with someone, then sat on my floor really upset for a while, then went to take a shower and started crying in there, then started laughing because who besides for random losers cries in the shower over absolutely nothing. So now I'll tell you why/what I'm having the hardest time getting over.

I hate the fact that I was who I was for the last few years. I know you always say that I needed to be like that so that I could become the me I am now, but this stuff kills me. I'm not kidding. It kills me that G-d gave me the ability to do so many things relatively easily and effortlessly, the dumbest things that are so not a big deal, sports, singing, painting, whatever and, not that I'm not grateful (I am), but why is it that the things that matter most don't come naturally, or didn't come naturally *at all* and I gotta sit there driving myself nuts thinking about them? It just seems strange and kind of dumb that it took me so long to apply myself to do some basic things when everything else came so effortlessly I'm not explaining myself but it's just so stupid and uch, I can't deal.

And the thing that really drives me crazy is hearing these girls in the school hallways — ninth or tenth graders mainly — say certain things or tell their friends about certain things and I KNOW one day they'll regret everything SO much and it's gonna be insanely hard for them to deal with it — just like me — and there's nothing I can do about it.

And I know you think I'm acting like I'm thirty and I should stop regretting things because the past is just that, but it SO matters to me. Not because I think I can't change things, *duh,* I can and did and will. And not because it means I'll never be okay with it, because I think (hope) that one day I'll make peace with it. But that doesn't make me feel any better that I was an idiot — it just doesn't. I hate that I wasn't as strong as I could have been when I should have been, and that I'll always have stories I don't want to have and I'll always know people I shouldn't have known and seen things I don't want to have seen. And it's not like anyone is gaining from my experiences, or growing from them, or learning anything or changing because of them. So right now, it's just a whole load of wasted time and I can't stand it. And the guiltier I feel, you would think it would push me to keep up with everything and make me stronger and more encouraged, but it really, really doesn't, it's just discouraging because as hard as I try I can't erase the past so what's the point...

It stinks. I know, I'm not going to let it pull me down now, blah, blah, blah, but it really gets to me. Especially when I get these random calls from people I really wish I never knew and I have to find some not-too-obnoxious way to tell them to lose my number. I'm sick of this.

Sarah

You know, it's a really big pressure to be someone else's role model. A couple of kids who are a year older than me were in my neighborhood for Shabbos. I happen to be really friendly with them; I always looked up to them for their strength in *tznius* and other Jewish areas, etc. Obviously, every time I saw them over Shabbos they were dressed perfectly *tznius* in terms of their necklines, knees, and all that, but neither wore tights. I, who of course assumed both of them would be wearing tights, was wearing them the whole Shabbos. But, on Saturday night I was faced with a dilemma.

So do *I* need to wear tights? And of course, that's the problem with having a role model. That's the problem with the "good" peer pressure: if you set everything you do by someone else's standards, what happens when they mess up? If someone is your role model, everything they do automatically becomes okay for you. So what happens if they are doing something you feel isn't, or shouldn't be, okay for them?

I realize now the danger here. When I was giving you such a hard time at the meeting, saying you were exaggerating how much people base their actions on what other people do, I don't think I was thinking about it like this. If even one girl in a room of twenty is looking at me, or cares what I'm doing, how could I let her down? I don't think this kid knew she was a role model for me; and she certainly would've been surprised/upset if she knew she had let me down. But she did. Because you really never know who's watching you. And with that thought I pulled on my tights.

Turned out both of them were wearing tights that night also. I guess it just looked good with what they were wearing. They're still awesome kids btw.

• • •

❤ Avigail

Okay, can I just throw something weird out there? It's much, much harder to dress *tznius* when you're not a size four. There are things that look fine on some people but totally awful on others, and it's not really fair. Sometimes I get this crazy urge to tap someone on the shoulder and say, "You know, the size up would probably look much better on you."

Don't worry, I suppress the urge. So far.

⭐ Chavi

You know those days when you just need to get outside? Like, it's Shabbos afternoon and it's BEAUTIFUL out and you just want to feel the air on your face? So you get up, but then you realize that you have nothing to do outside. You suddenly wish you were a kid again, going out to play, or young enough not to need an excuse to go outside by yourself for a while. For some reason, you just can't go out by yourself to take a huge, thought-filled walk — at least, I can't. I just feel too weird about it. So I end up staring out the window all day, wishing I could enjoy the weather from where it comes from — outside. What I'm trying to say is that being passive because of self-consciousness is not a good thing. I guess I would even say it's a terrible thing.

Doing something out of the norm is character building. It proves you're strong, different, and that you have the courage to stand apart — literally. You can't live your life thinking, "I can't do this or that because people might think I'm off my rocker," because sometimes, you need to veer off the track of conformity and head into a life you know is right. Sometimes, you *need* those solitary walks, sometimes that's just what makes you, you. Because how can you know what's you if you're always trying to be someone else? So get out and stride around your neighborhood with pride and passion and enthusiasm. You are a thinking Jew, and there's nothing better to be.

That's something I'm working on right now. I want to really engrave it into my head so I never doubt myself. Because if you start freaking out on top of a cable-wire bridge hundreds of feet off the ground, it's SO hard to get that initial confidence back and...then what? You're scared out your mind, stuck halfway through the sky with nowhere to go — SO MOVE ON. Just finish what you started and don't let other people get in the way of you conquering your fear of heights.

✿ Rachel

In eighth grade, I was really into hanging out with the "cool kids" who were friends with all the boys. I had my good friends that I grew up with, but I was always willing to do anything to get into the other scene.

So for a birthday/graduation party, one of my good friends made a pool party at her house with a barbecue. I went and hung out at the pool first with my friends, and then I went inside to where all the cool kids were sitting. Two of them wanted to meet up with a group of guys at a pizza place later, so we all decided not to eat the food that my friend's mom stood there barbecuing (we said we weren't hungry). Oh, and side point: — my mom didn't let me go out with boys. Ever.

Anyway, so we had this plan. After ditching my real friends the entire time, we asked a girl (who didn't really have any friends — basically, we took disgusting advantage of her) if her mom could drop us off at the pizza place on the way home. So we got our ride taken care of, and I called my mom to tell her I wouldn't be coming straight home and she shouldn't worry. Well, she's not slow and of course she asked like a thousand questions, but I finally got her off the phone. So we got to the pizza place, and before we even get the food, my mother shows up, screams at me in front of everyone for about five minutes about how dishonest I was and how many people I had hurt and all that. I was beyond embarrassed. These were all the cool kids — and now I looked like the biggest loser in the world. I followed my mom to the car and every single kid's eyes followed me.

I screamed at my mother the whole way home, crying and mortified, sure that my life was over. When we got home, both my parents sat me down for a long talk about peer pressure, and how I had ditched my real friends, lied to my mother, and hung out with kids who they didn't approve of. I sobbed through the entire lecture, and then I got my punishment. I was grounded indefinitely, and I had to go over to my friend's house to apologize to her and her mom. I was crying through the apologies also, the entire experience was mortifying and degrading. But — I know this sounds crazy — I will never be able to thank my parents enough for what they did. Since then, the scare factor of that memory makes me so much more conscious of peer pressure. I remember the embarrassment and the terrible guilt. I'm still friends with that girl today, and it kills me that she for sure remembers that awful party and my involvement in it.

♪ Ellie

My neighbor who's a couple of years younger than me was going to Lakewood for Shabbos, and she wanted to make sure everything she was going to be wearing was super okay, so she came over just now to borrow clothes from ME. I know it's more convenience than being actually qualified to borrow from, but it was still an amazing thing. It just felt so good and made everything so worth it. It's just sometimes so hard to see yourself how others perceive you, but a good place to start is by analyzing how other people act around you, because that's based on the type of attitude or aura you (me) give off. I just stopped making sense. Sometimes I get into these moods where I get totally defensive, and other times I get so weighed down by guilt for the past, but tonight — just because some kid asked for a stupid outfit to wear — was an awesome breath of fresh air and a good start on a better attitude.

Sarah

So you know how I always have this thing with it being too early to change the way I dress now, like, I have lots of time to be busy with those sort of things and no one else is doing it, so why should I?

So I was talking to someone recently, and she was saying a lot of smart things about it. I was telling her that it's hard to change, because sometimes I feel like I'm the only one who's into these things, and she was like hello, nice to meet you, my name is _____, I'm also into it, and I actually think it's better that none of your friends are into changing in this way right now, because then you know you're doing this for the right reasons. So, *I* said, ha ha my name's Sarah, and I totally agree but I keep thinking it's different because I'm so much younger than you. And *she* said, that's true but it's also better once you establish yourself as a certain type of kid — the type who thinks about these things. It's so much easier because your friends get used to it, as opposed to them waking up one day and being like — whoa, what's with *you*? You know?

And that's true. I am trying to make friends who will grow with me, but it's hard. And then she said something that was really powerful — maybe just because of who she is. She said — well, you have to put things in perspective. Hashem is more important than your friends. And she also said that in a way, she was going through the same thing. And that sometimes you only find out who your real friends are after you go through something like this.

And I agree. It's better to make the changes now, and establish myself as the person I want to be, rather than kid the people around me until I'm brave enough to finally take action. So yeah, maybe the girls I think I want to be friends with won't really understand how I'm acting, and maybe it will be harder to grow and maintain certain friendships while I'm trying to figure all this stuff out, but at least I'm getting a head start now, and the friends that I do make will be real and lasting and positive for me. It's funny, because now it seems so obvious, but wow, I just never thought about it like this before.

● ● ●

♡ Avigail

I've noticed that depending on who I'm with, my feelings about *tznius*, as well as some other *middos* of mine, really change. I have this one friend who's struggling now with a bunch of different things, and for some strange reason, whenever I'm around her, I feel like everything is such a burden. Also, whenever I finish watching a certain TV show, or watch certain types of movies, my whole language changes. Well, that's kind of an obvious one, but I think it's time to do something about that.

Lately I find myself thinking about *bushah* a lot. I've noticed how just nothing seems to phase me anymore, and that's kind of sad. Is it possible to get *bushah* back? To train yourself to get more sensitive to these things?

☆ Chavi

I'm getting really annoyed at the girl who keeps yelling at me to stop judging her and stuff. She says something like this at least once a day, and whenever she hears me use like a not such a nice word or something, she jumps down my throat and makes this huge deal out of it. Recently, she reminded the whole class about all of the different friends that I used to have and I was laughing along with everyone else, but really, why does she feel that the only thing she can talk to me about is how much I changed? I'm still me.

❀ Rachel

I have such respect for the freshmen in this group. I look back at myself in ninth grade and remember how I thought and acted, and I can't even imagine being so serious about growth and self-improvement with *tznius* — I was so into making new friends, being cool, etc.

— I never even thought about *tznius* until that summer. But I look at them, and they're unbelievable! It's not even like they have their own money, or are able to drive to a mall to get new clothes or anything. It sounds like no big deal, but it is so, so much harder to make these changes when you're so dependent on other people.

Shevi

On Sunday I went out with a couple of old friends. I wore a shorter skirt than I normally wear, and a lower neckline also. I just wanted to look like them, I guess. It was dumb. I felt like I was wearing a costume, and when I passed my reflection in a store window, I was confused. I really didn't feel like it was me. Uch.

Ellie

So, I'm in my sister's room and she was trying on a new shirt. She goes, "Is this too tight?" Well, it was snug, but she's so skinny, you really can't tell. So I go "I don't know," and then she's like, "Well, would *you* wear it?"

Whoa.

Suddenly, I realized that she really values my opinion. I mean, not my opinion so much as my boundaries, you know? I'm not sure how to explain this, it's like she bases things on what I would do.

Well, now that I'm thinking about it, it's like duh — that's what sisters do, I guess. I'm not sure why it came as such a shock. But now...I don't know, it's like, that's a HUGE responsibility! This means that when I choose to do, or not to do something, really I'm not just choosing for myself. I don't really love responsibility all that much, but I do love my sister, and I guess I owe it to her in a way. And also to myself, so she can be what I wasn't at her age. Okay, I must get some sleep now.

Sarah

I'm getting really annoyed because my friends keep telling me that we need to work on an English project and of course the one night that works for them is the night that we're meeting, so I told them, and they're all like, "Omgsh, can't you just miss one stupid meeting? This is so much more important!"

Yeah, they *would* think that.

MARCH

Ins and Outs of Dressing Up

THE SIXTH MEETING

n March, we read out loud parts of everyone's journals again. The scene was similar to the first time I did this (the self-conscious faces, the embarrassed comments), but something about the dynamic of the group was changed. They were more receptive to the ideas; they were more open-minded to what the other girls were writing about.

I took advantage of the mood to talk about different areas of *tznius* that ordinarily I wouldn't have brought up. Levels and sensitivities are something a person is most ready for when she comes to them on her own. That said, I did want the girls to start thinking about things they hadn't thought about before.

So we discussed dancing, makeup, movies, language. We spoke about specific style shirts and skirts, looks that left a bad taste though nothing was obviously wrong with them. Actions that didn't conform to the spirit of the *halachos*.

It was the first time I felt like they were really getting the ideas behind the principles of *tznius*. It wasn't that they were dramatically (or even subtly) changing their lives (though some were), it was more that they were finally appreciating *tznius* for what it was, and they were able to hold onto the details of halachah while keeping the broader importance of the mitzvah as a whole.

I wasn't sure when or how this change had come about, but it was heartening to see.

• • •

♡ Avigail

So...there it was — the perfect dress — well, almost perfect. It was *so* cute. I tried it on and it fit perfectly and it was so *tznius* and then I found ten more perfect dresses and the Arabs made peace with Israel and we all lived happily ever after.

Yeah, it was too short.

Duh.

So I got a bigger size and now it looks weirdish on top and at the waist but it's a little longer. The thing is — it's still a bit short. But it's so cute. (But I didn't get this other too-short skirt, plus I got a good black, perfectly *tznius* skirt. I don't know when I'll ever wear it, but whatever.)

What do I do?! I love the dress and I know it's wrong. My mom hasn't seen it yet, probably never will. Last time I tried to talk to her about this stuff she started screaming and yelling. Duh, that's as obvious as the dress length and world peace.

Why do they get so irrationally upset? I hate never being able to answer back anything, because everything I say is considered "disrespectful." I really don't want to be like that when I grow up. I want to be great, amazing, understanding...

And this is not what I'm supposed to be writing about.

Okay, so you know those moments of total clarity? Like, when you know that it's all so true and right, and everything else is wrong. It's all just so clear. So those moments...I wish there was a way to just preserve them, you know? And like, live it. Your whole life — with that complete, deep understanding. With nothing in the way. That would be nice.

☆ Chavi

Do you know I can't stand pictures? I know, that was really random, but I just find them so irritating. I just don't see the point half the time, they just make me feel clicky and shallow and vain. And people think I'm weird and they sometimes just forget I was there because I'm not that person who jumps into all the shots. I feel like that can fall under *tznius* in actions.

❀ Rachel

So I know this kid who's a really great girl, so kind-hearted and caring, and she also dresses very *tznius*. But to me, I forget all of that when I hear her talk and laugh. When she talks, she talks in this really loud voice, and speaks over whoever happens to be speaking at the time. In a way, I think she needs everyone to hear her, see her, notice her — she just seems to be so attention-grabbing. The way she acts seems to contradict the way she dresses. *Tznius* to me is a package deal — you really have to have it all. *Tznius* is a mentality and an awareness — a constant awareness of how you dress, talk, stand, think, and feel. In my mind, that means someone who is completely self-aware. That's the goal, anyway.

✎ Shevi

Something happened to me on Shabbos that taught me a lesson on judging people by what they wear. I went someplace for Shabbos, and while we were in shul, I was standing with my group of friends talking (not during *davening*, obviously) and one of them goes, "Shevi, don't turn around." Well, of course I turn around and I see this lady and *her* whole group of friends all staring at me. I'm not exaggerating, they were looking at me up and down with the snobbiest looks, I don't know, one of them must have commented to the others about something I was wearing.

I was really taken aback. I don't know why I automatically felt so guilty — there was nothing wrong with what I was wearing, but it was like... I automatically went into defensive mode. I don't know what those ladies' issues were. People like that make me nauseous. She may have been dressed totally *tznius*, but, seriously, sometimes other things count, too.

♪ Ellie

As a rule, I wear tights during the week, but on *motza'ei Shabbos/* Sunday I don't make myself because...whatever. After wearing them all week, I'll admit that it feels strange not wearing them then, but that's just what I do.

So today I woke up late and realized that class was starting in ten minutes. I threw on whatever was lying around my room, and I couldn't find tights *anywhere*. I just ended up pulling on a pair of short socks and Naot and left the house. Walking to school was fine, but as soon as I got to my classroom, even though no one could care less what's on my legs, I went straight to my desk and curled my legs under my chair — and sat like that for the entire day! I don't know why, it's not like I wear them *all* the time and I'm certainly not ready or willing to commit to start, but for some reason I just felt so naked without them! I have nothing really deep to say about the whole story, but it was really strange.

✎ Sarah

Rachel is an amazing human being. I used to think that she was just this totally naturally *frum* person who spoke softly and dressed *tznius* and I don't know. Okay, that was a dumb thing to say, but I guess what I mean is that I never really knew that much about her. Now that I got to know her I also know her amazing personality and all that...

I went to her house this past weekend, and just looking at all her photo albums and stuff I realize how insanely strong she must have been, and still is, to have made all the changes that she did, even though they make her stick out so obviously from the rest of her family. She goes to the beach with everyone and doesn't budge from her standards one drop — just sits there in her skirt and long-sleeve tee-shirt while everyone is in bathing suits. And just talking to her and seeing how she acts and thinks and dresses totally inspires me. She's just great.

It was weird because the skirt that I wore on Shabbos kept riding up, and I kept having to pull it down, and every time it did I kept glancing at her, embarrassed. But not because she's *frummer* than me and made me feel stupid — not at all. It's cuz I come from parents with all these really religious *hashkafos* and standards, and I still feel like I'm so far behind where I should be in *tznius*. And meanwhile, she's been changing and growing and being who she is with no family support. And I keep wishing my mother would stop nagging me about certain shirts and skirts before I leave the house each day.

And yeah. So that's all for now.

• • •

♡ Avigail

I want to grow, I really do. It's who I am. Why is the physical so hard to get past? Why does it have to be such a strong obstacle? How come it seems like there are some girls that Judaism comes so easily to?

I feel like it's easier once you get married — is it? There's the answer to all my problems. Somehow, I don't think that would sit well with my parents. Then again, nothing really sits well with them. Okay, that's a little harsh.

Okay, ugh, you realize I, like, totally write my thoughts. Like, word for word. Is that annoying? I feel like it's a one-sided dialogue.

I can't focus. I'll write a different time.

☆ Chavi

When I look at what other girls wear, specifically the girls who dress how I used to, I don't feel very different. I know maybe my skirts are longer, but even though I don't do the whole Hollister/ Abercrombie uniform anymore, I don't feel so different. I still wear the same *style* stuff, so it's not a big deal, but at the same time, it is. I don't know when exactly I stopped wearing all the Holl-Ab stuff I've been amassing since seventh grade; I guess I just grew out of it. And with the other stuff, well you told us the *halachos*, and I guess I know it's the right thing to do, so I follow it — I bought longer skirts, and my sweaters are not as tight, and I try not to wear words anymore, but I still feel like me, you know? I don't feel like, yeah, I'm a totally different person now, because I'm not. Am I doing something wrong? Am I supposed to feel totally different? Or *am* I different, just a different *me*?

Today a girl in school told me I inspire her, and that's really weird because I don't feel like that type of person at all. When I think of inspiring people, I think of like a *ba'alas teshuvah* or something. Not some kid who's still confused by all the inconsistent, vague messages she's been getting at home. The only thing consistent about my parents' rules of dress is their inconsistency. I think I like rules — not the annoying stupid ones, but the real ones that make sense. I get it: I get what I have to do for *tznius*, and it's logical. Baseless rules get on my nerves. I think that's why I love math and science so much. Things shouldn't and don't come from nowhere for some random reason nobody knows about. I've been told so many wrong things about *tznius* that when I hear the right thing, I have no doubts. It's like this internal lie detector.

Rachel

It's actually taking me a really long time to pack for school Shabbos because I really don't want to take along any questionable clothing. I just don't want anyone to look at my clothes and say, "Oh, so it's okay to wear that, because she is." It scares me a lot.

Shevi

After the last meeting we had I was all fired up and *had* to do something. I looked in my closet and saw my perfect shade, unbelievably comfortable, too-short jean skirt hanging there, waiting for me to decide what to do with it. I had three choices:

1. Wear the skirt even though it's slightly tight, *just* covers my knee, and has a slit up the back.
2. Keep it in my closet so that it begs me to wear it every single morning.
3. Get rid of it.

So I knew exactly what I needed to do. I took out the skirt, and grabbed my markers, and started coloring *all* over it! The second that red marker touched the skirt, I felt so amazing and so free! I was really proud of myself. (As I was coloring, I was like, venting out on the skirt: how long it took me to do this, and how awesome it was that it could never tempt me again... I wrote down all my reasons. It was cool.)

Then I took a pair of scissors, and cut the skirt down the front, because I realized the markers were washable!

♪ Ellie

So I was going through a friend's notes from classes I missed (cut), and she happens to be pretty good at drawing, and I noticed that all her doodles were of *tznius* stuff. Which was pretty cool to see how sensitive she was about it...but is it an issue if someone doesn't always draw like that?

Maybe it's just a reflection of what someone considers appropriate...or maybe it's just a sensitivity thing — but either way, it was nice to see.

I guess if the people around us are constantly dressed in a provocative way, then we get used to it and see it as the norm — and forget that we shouldn't consider it normal, but dysfunctional.

 Sarah

So I've been wearing tights every day now, and even though I've been doing it as a step up in *tznius*, I can't help but feel like I'm lying to myself. Whenever someone says to me, "You wear tights everyday?" I just go, "Yeah," and kind of giggle. Like, yeah, I know I'm *frum* like that. Even though I know I'm not, and the truth is that I'm only wearing tights because it's freezing outside. Plus, it's not even considered nerdy, because for some reason, everyone is wearing them, they're considered like "in" or something. So I'm wondering if I'm going to be strong enough to wear tights even after the winter.

Strong is not really the right word. It's just that now I feel like I have this *kabbalah*, and I feel good about myself, like, k, I'm really actively working on my clothing! So I kind of feeling like I'm "good" right now, which basically means DANGER ZONE!!

Cuz when you're in a situation where you feel like you're in control, that's when you're totally not. That is when the *yetzer hara* is in control. All of a sudden, it's like a free-pass card — like, yeah, if I do something wrong or not totally kosher, it's okay, because I'm wearing tights. Or something like that. And it becomes harder to be harsh on myself for something I'm doing wrong, or something that I know is beneath me, because it's like hey, give me a break — I'm working on *tznius*! So I think it's really important to strike a balance. Duh, everyone wants to feel good and accomplished, but at the end of the day, you can't say that it's fine that I'm not _____, or _____, because hey, I'm wearing longer skirts! I'm wearing tights! I'm working on *tznius*!

Sure you are. But is it cuz you're working on it, or because you're looking for a justification to get out of all the other things you're *not* working on?

• • •

♡ Avigail

Wow. School Shabbos. Yeah, I wore the dress. And yeah, it was short. And yeah, I felt cute and uncomfortable at the same time. And I have no idea when or if I'll ever wear it again. But that's not what I want to write about.

Outside of the school hallways, you get to see another side of all the kids in your grade. And sometimes I'm like...wow. And other times I'm like...ew.

If someone walks around the room, wearing very little — even when there are only girls around — I don't know. What does that say about her? To me, it doesn't exactly scream self-respect. I mean, I know she's a nice kid, but that part of her personality is just, well, gross. I don't know why kids do these types of things. Shock value? Or do they just honestly feel like these things are no big deal, like, just chill out and stop being so uptight and *frum* about everything?

I feel so bad for them.

☆ Chavi

A lot of things happened this Shabbos that caught my attention, but I really wanted to write about one specific thing.

Everyone could not stop making comparisons between this year and last year. We kept saying things like, well, last year we roomed with this group, and ate with that group. And last year we did this in the afternoon, and do you remember who you called the second Shabbos was over, and all that junk. And last year you were wearing...and on and on and on.

And it's a funny thing. I know I sound schizo on this, but remember how I kept saying that I don't feel like a different person than before? I lied. I totally do. I'm just not sure when or how it happened.

❋ Rachel

I love that I'm at the point in my life where I'm comfortable with my friends and my *frumkeit* and everything else. Looking around on Shabbos at everybody looking at everyone else, and self-consciously checking themselves out to make sure they looked okay...uch. I think it would be a lie to say I'm totally past that, because I don't think you ever get past wanting to look good and fit in, but I'm glad that I'm not so dependent on other people's opinions. I just want to feel pretty and dress according to halachah. I think those are my two constant criteria for clothing: is this halachically okay, and do I feel pretty in it? Because feeling like you look good is so important — I hate when people say that they just don't feel pretty when they wear *tznius* clothes. So then just buy different ones in a different style! The only time dressing *tznius* looks nerdy is if you're a nerd. It is possible to be cool and dress *tznius*. It may be harder to pull off, but so what?

Shevi

Is it just me, or do girls wear a lot more makeup than they should? I'm not even talking *tznius*-wise, though obviously it's not exactly fine-looking to line your eyes in kohl black and walk around with a heavy layer of lip gloss. But it's not just that... I just think it looks weird. Like, hello, you're fifteen years old. What's with the face full of makeup at nine thirty in the morning on some random Wednesday? I know girls who will not leave the house without some eye makeup. It's so pathetic. Why can't you just let yourself be a kid? And even on Shabbos... C'mon, where d'you think you're going? A little goes a long way. Chill.

Thanks, I feel better now.

Ellie

What a CRAZY night. Omgsh — k, I'll start from the beginning. A really, really long time ago, I pulled tons of clothes out of my closet, and made this massive pile in the hallway where I went through everything. I threw out most of it and kept some as pj's. Anyway, that was a while ago and much has happened since then, and it was time for another clean sweep. Eleven shirts, five skirts, two sweaters and a dress later, my closet is one step closer to helping me be a *tzanua* person.

It's a crazy thing, though. Even though I loved what I was doing — it felt great and liberating in a way — subconsciously, I kept tallying up the amount of money spent on each article of clothing being thrown out. I really don't care about the money if it's the right thing, but thinking I could've just spent the money on the right clothing in the first place...what a waste! Plus, what in the world am I supposed to wear?!

And then it hit me. Lately, I've been getting money from the most random places — like being paid back money I lent to people *ages* ago, or getting paid for youth groups I did a while ago, babysitting jobs, etc., etc. Well, the money isn't suddenly pouring in now for no reason! It's just so crazy how Hashem makes everything work out in every situation. I know it sounds cheesy, especially from a kid, but I see it all the time. I think it's an amazing thing. Once a person decides to work on *tznius* despite the obstacles, Hashem then opens up opportunities to make it easier. I find it funny in a way. Like, we all claim to believe in Hashem, but very few of us actually keep it in mind when thinking of His involvement with our daily lives. It's a crazy thing, no?

 # Sarah

School Shabbos was amazing, and as far as dress goes, I don't have all that much to say, but I did notice a couple of things having to do with *tznius* in thoughts and actions.

I chose to room with kids who I just became friendly with like a few weeks ago, as opposed to with my old group, who I'm still friends with, but...I don't know. It's not that I want to leave my old group of friends, because I don't, it's just that I guess I wanted to see what things would be like with different girls, who are more open-ly focused on growing and things like that. Well, it ended up being great, and I had a great time, except for these little pangs of...I guess jealousy here and there, whenever I saw the whole group having fun without me. It's just weird because I'm so used to hanging with them...not that they cared. But overall, I was glad that I stepped out of my comfort zone. I just think it's important to be friends with other types of kids. And while some girls spent the whole Friday night trying on each other's clothes, running up and down the hallways singing all these songs, and talking about anything and everything that shouldn't necessarily be talked about, I spent it talking about issues that mean a lot to me, and playing fun, random games and having a *kumzitz* at three a.m. with a bunch of girls I would never ordinarily hang with. So yeah, it wasn't what I usually do, but I had a really good time.

And I think it has a lot to do with *tznius*. I mean, when you (I) spend so much time thinking about and talking about all these things, and how our outsides should reflect our insides and about our *neshamah* and being true to it and all that, I can't help but want to spend my time differently. And it was hard because then things got awkward with my friends in school because it was obvious that I had distanced myself a little bit, but it was worth it. Hearing some kids bragging about how they skipped the workshops, and slept through the speeches, and they're all like "yeah, we're cool like that," and I was just looking at them like, sorry, your loss. In their minds, they had a good time, and that's what counts. But it's not. At least, not in my opinion.

• • •

♥ Avigail

Purim. What a crash down.

I love dressing up. I do, I always did, and I don't think there's anything wrong with that. But why is it that it's so easy to get carried away with it? It's hard to explain, but when I was dressed up, it was just all wrong. I felt people staring at me, I knew I was getting a lot of not-such-good attention, and I loved it and felt guilty/wrong all at the same time.

But what bothers me most, now that I'm back to my non-costumed self is, which is the real me? The girl who dressed up, totally overdoing it and liking it, or the girl who knows I just used Purim as an excuse to take a break from the spirit of the law? I know that they're both me to an extent, but I do hope that by next Purim I won't even have the desire to do anything like that again. I don't want people thinking of me like that.

I look at some kids in school, and you can see how special and good they are. It just shines out clearly. I want people to see me like that.

☆ Chavi

I keep getting these mixed messages from my parents. Sometimes, I don't even think it's about me trying to be more *tznius*. I think it's about me changing — threatening them and their level of Judaism and the decisions they made in their own lives. They just can't let me take my own road.

Today I went to a dressmaker to make up something to wear to my cousin's wedding. She mentioned how she works with a lot of *frum* people, though she herself isn't Jewish. She asked me if I want it to cover my elbows, and I said yes, but I don't care if it had long sleeves or three-quarter sleeves. I was also asked how high I wanted the neck to be, so I told her I wanted it to cover my collarbone. Then my mom jumped in and she started getting all frantic about how that's too high, and I could get it just under, it would look so much better and blah, blah, blah. Well, I wasn't up for the fight, so I just gave in.

I don't know if it's a huge deal for one night, but there are so many pictures to take, I know I'll feel awkward. The lady was telling me how it's okay to have it that low, because a lot of *frum* ladies have their clothing made that low, and it's fine. What was I supposed to say? That they're wrong?

❀ Rachel

Tonight was my brother's bar mitzvah, and it was really nice. At one point, I was watching a whole bunch of my relatives/family friends, and normally I would have been sitting with them, just chilling out, but for some reason, I just wasn't, and you get a different perspective when you're not actually a part of the scene.

Don't get me wrong, it's not like anyone was doing anything wrong, but still... Like when there's this cute little throwing fight that starts out with spitting grapes and then all of a sudden he's threatening to spill a whole glass of soda on her dress...you know what I mean? These people aren't even related. I don't know, it just rubbed me wrong.

I'm wearing this really nerdy pink nail polish, because my mom made me get a manicure for the bar mitzvah. I stopped wearing nail polish ages ago because I only like the really, really dark colors. I still think it's cool, but it attracts too much attention, I'm just not comfortable with it.

Shevi

Okay, something I've been thinking: so, B"H I feel myself thinking about Hashem so much more in my daily life. A lot of times when I'm doing something, the thought will pop into my head: Is this good for my *neshamah*? Is this good for my relationship with Him? And I really feel like it helps me make the right decisions!

Am I weird?

Ellie

Today a friend of mine asked me why I care more about *tznius* than my family does. Like, why do I do things even though my parents don't make me and stuff. Thank G-d the teacher walked in at that second, because I seriously don't know what I would have told her.

First of all, I hate explaining to people why I do what I do, especially because I barely have a clue myself. I know I do things because I feel that Hashem wants me to, I mean, obviously that's a biggie. And I know it has amazing benefits for me, so that too. But there's no question that these reasons/values aren't on my mind every second. So what about the moments when the whole thing stinks, and I just wanna run outside to the neighbors without doing a whole *tznius* check, or I just want to fool around in the mall or be loud in the street because it's fun to not think about what I'm doing every single second?

I guess choices turn into habits and then into a way of life. I guess this just became the norm for me.

So is that how and why I keep it up? Because it became the norm?! I don't want it to become the norm, I want to feel good about it every time. If it gets too old and routine then...then...then, yeah. Well, that went nowhere. Hope she doesn't ask again.

Oh, and you know when you were talking about the whole lip gloss thing at the meeting and I kept saying that I didn't get it? I was lying. I really do.

Sarah

I'm wondering if what you choose to dress up as on Purim says anything about you. I mean, I think it does. Not that like, if you dress up Goth, it means that you secretly want to be Goth. But if you think that dressing up a certain way is cool, then yeah, I think it does say something about you.

I don't think *v'nahapoch hu* means to dress up as the opposite of all of your morals and values. I think it means to dress up as something unusual or unexpected. Or as a different person, whatever floats your boat. But dressing up as someone lacking in *tznius*, if you're usually good in this area, should *not* float your boat.

APRIL

Boys — Where Do We Draw the Line?

THE SEVENTH MEETING

Well, here was a topic I didn't want to discuss. I had never intended to discuss boys with them, for many reasons. I wanted to present *tznius* in a way that had nothing to do with guys; I wanted to broaden their horizons and get them thinking about the other ways *tznius* affects their day-to-day lives. That said, I was deluding myself about how big a role boys played in their lives. It became apparent from their journals that boys were a very big part of their *nisayon* of *tznius*, and I didn't feel like it would behoove them for me to stay with my head in the sand. In general, I think we owe it to our girls to deal directly with the issues they struggle with, as opposed to pretending they live in the world we'd like them to be living in.

One of the reasons why I dislike discussing boys in general was the first thing we discussed that night: you cannot talk to a girl who has friends that are boys about the topic without her saying things that are completely moronic. For some reason, there are bright, strong girls who just can't seem to think straight when the topic is boys. (This has got to be scientifically brought down somewhere. Kids are constantly telling me about their capable, funny friends who are reduced to giggling lumps of Jello when within a two-foot radius of a breathing boy.) Which is also why you end up hearing girls say hysterical things like, "Are you *shomer*?" (said from one friend to another, as if it's an option, as in "Do you eat *gebrokst*?"). Or, "We're just casual friends, it's not going anywhere." Or, "I'll go there/hang with them, but I won't talk to the boys." It's hard to argue with this kind of (il)logic. In this topic, the heart seems to lead the head, and until a girl is removed from the situation, it's difficult for her to be completely honest or self-aware. Which is a problem, because it is in this area that a kid can fall so, so far so, so fast.

For the most part, the girls were much more receptive than I thought they would be, maybe because it was after seven months of focusing on these issues. In general, I found myself surprised by how open they were to hearing a new side to ideas they had taken for granted until now. It made me wonder about all of the times adults hold back from sharing things with kids because they assume they're not ready to accept them. Is there any group that is more consistently underestimated than teenagers?

• • •

♥ Avigail

I was just on the phone with a girl I used to be really close with — I guess we still are close, but in a different way. She was crying to me about a boy that she was best friends with, but has been fighting with for over a year. For over a year I've been trying to tell her to forget him because he isn't worth it. I'm SO happy that I don't have to deal with any of this garbage anymore. She told me that her guy friends make her who she is. I just find it so ironic that the same guys who get her so emotionally messed up, make her who she is. I just think it's funny how girls don't realize how stupid they sound when they talk about boys.

☆ Chavi

Disorientation is a funny thing. Like when you walk into an ice-cream store and ask for a mint chocolate-chip milk shake. So you stand at the counter while Dave, the ice-cream guy, puts it in the blender, and you're looking around because you don't want to get caught staring intently at the ice cream spinning around. Dave says, "Excuse me," and you snap out of your random thoughts and take a good hard look at the milk shake. Something is not right. It turns out, your dream milk shake, is, WHITE MINT! Before you can even think *ew!* you shoot Dave this nasty look, like, "Are you trying to kill me?" Of course you never specified green mint, but who would *ever* ask for white mint? It makes you uncomfortable seeing the white cuz you're so used to the green. You're disoriented. Of course, that's a little extreme, but how can you *not* be extreme when you're dealing with a white-mint, chocolate-chip milkshake?

This little-too extended metaphor is headed somewhere, I promise. So when I sit on the bus, I'm glued to my seat for about an hour going home — that's a long time. So I start off sitting regular, with my feet on the floor like you are supposed to, then fifteen minutes into the ride I lean my knees on the seat in front of me, with my head really low down. Which makes my skirt move to *way* above my knees. I used to just leave it there — what's the big deal about knees showing on a school bus full of girls? Well, for some super odd reason, I have not been comfortable with my knees showing on the bus. I know it's weird, but I get all disoriented and I'm like, "uhh..." I just feel the need to pull my skirt so it's good when I'm sitting like that. So you see the white shake, or your knees showing and you're like, "Whoa, I didn't ask for that!" So you pull it down, even if it's uncomfortable, or you ask Dave to make you a new one even if you sound stupid. Because you want what you ordered.

Rachel

Up until a few months ago, I was reading a lot of books — and many of them were not the most appropriate books out there. I always knew there was a problem with it, but I never let myself stop. I rationalized that (1) I'm amazing for reading anything at all — it's good for my vocabulary; and (2) better to spend my time reading this, than watching things on TV. I was seriously hooked on these books. Honestly, I don't know what made me stop — maybe it was all the school work — but for a few months I stopped reading and I seriously cannot believe what a difference it made. I can't really describe it but I feel like something was restored. I know this doesn't make sense, and I don't know if it's possible to get back what I lost when I started reading those kinds of books, but something did come back. So I went through all of my books, and got rid of all the inappropriate ones before I lost the...inspiration, I guess you'd call it. I honestly don't want to read books like that again, now that I see that they have such a real effect on me.

Shevi

I went bowling this past Sunday night, and wore short socks because I thought it would be more comfortable without annoying tights, which would also look so nerdy with bowling shoes. The last time I went bowling with my friends, everyone was making so much fun of how I looked.

It was a mistake. What I thought would make me feel more comfortable, ended up making me feel awful. I've been working so hard this year to start covering my legs all the time — even my mother said to me before I left, "Are you sure you want to go out without stockings?" Like an idiot I said yes, and I walked out the door.

♪ Ellie

The first time I went to the Kosel and saw all the different types of Jewish women standing there *davening*, I immediately felt a sense of *kedushah*. I started to daven *Minchah* and was so inspired to be better, *do* better, and want more of a connection to Hashem.

The problem was, I was wearing a half-sleeve shirt, a jean skirt that "covered my knees," and open-toed Naot. My shirt barely covered my collarbone and my hair was really long and crazy. Suddenly, though there were people all around me that were definitely less covered than I was, I just felt...unholy. A second before, I was so uplifted and inspired, and now I was so discouraged. My insides and my outsides were so far apart, it just ruined the whole experience.

Sarah

I think that *bushah* is the natural shame in everyone, the natural instinct people have to cover up. It's that small voice that tells you, *this isn't me!* The alarm in your head that screams, "Wake up, wake up!" *Bushah* is what keeps us *tznius* in our actions, our speech, our dress — even in front of other girls. It's a built-in defense mechanism against the *yetzer hara*.

When a curse flies out of our mouth, and we get this jolt, this feeling of, "Oops" — that's *bushah*. When we're at a sleepover, and a girl thinks it's cool to sit around wearing way too little, and everyone cringes even if some people end up doing it too — that's *bushah*. The vague feeling of "I really don't want to be here, even though I'm having fun" — that's *bushah*.

You told us to protect our *bushah*, because it's delicate and gets damaged quickly. My translation — be aware of it. Don't shrug it off as insecurity or discomfort. It's your *neshamah*'s way of hammering at the door you're locked behind.

I hear it. I'm up. Wide awake. I don't know why it took so long.

• • •

♥ Avigail

Last year I went to a school basketball game, and in school I wore a zip-up over an almost to the elbow shirt that I cut at the sides to make frillies with one night when I was bored. When I got to the game, I took off the zip-up. Aside from the fact that it had short sleeves, which is not what I usually wear, I also did a bad job of cutting the shirt, so it had some holes where you could see straight through.

I cared. I was uncomfortable. I waved to the teachers who were there like everything was normal. I was an idiot.

☆ Chavi

Okay, the weather is officially warmer. I thought that clear tights would be okay for spring, but they're not. I'm going to melt if I don't find some sort of balance between dressing *tznius* and not wearing fifteen layers.

Four girls (at least) asked me to donate my old clothes to them. I mean, HELLLOOOOO?! The only shirts I ever wear now are sweaters because I just can't seem to find a decent shirt out there. I need to go shopping, but I HATE it. Either I'm going to sweat for the whole rest of the year (hence the word "sweater"), or I'm gonna shiver — meaning, cheat myself out of what I've been working on all year. Well, honestly, if I had to choose between shiver and sweat, my answer would no doubt be SWEAT. Absolutely. I mean, hopefully I won't be in such a drastic position, but hey, you never know. Okay, so I'm not really in that position yet, so I don't know if I can say absolutely, and you also have to factor in peer pressure and stuff like looking weird but —

NO! *Forget* peer pressure. THIS SUMMER, I OFFICIALLY DE-CLARE THAT IF I'M IN A SHIVER/SWEAT PREDICAMENT, I SHALL ALWAYS ONLY CHOOSE SWEAT!!!!!!! (to be read with a lot of expression.)

Whoa. Glad to get that one official and out into the open. Thank you.

 # Rachel

So I was on the phone with a friend and we had plans to meet at the pizza place on Sunday. I was trying to find some shirt to throw on because I had just come back from practice, and I saw my Abercrombie boy's big sweater pullover. It looked like the perfect thing to wear to go out for like an hour. I didn't care about looking gross — I was so lazy and tired. But I'm not sure why, I just felt a little weird about it so I asked my friend what she thought. She's one of my best friends. Although she doesn't dress like me, or look at things the way I do, I asked her to think about me when she answered, and tell me if she thought it was something I should be wearing. I can't tell you how grateful I was that she answered me honestly. She said that even though she definitely doesn't see anything wrong with it, she'd be surprised to see me in it, because I usually look more...put together.

When I told this story to someone else, she stopped me in the middle and asked why I would ask her, if she always wears different types of clothes. So I told her that as a best friend, it's part of her job to tell me what I need to hear and to help me grow, regardless of where she is holding. So this kid was like, "Oh. I guess that makes sense. I don't know, my friendships aren't like that."

I never realized until then how important it is to have those kinds of friendships. I don't know what I would have done if I didn't have a good group of friends who supported me through all my changes. They helped me so much — and still do — even if it means just being there so I'm not the only one dressed or acting in a certain way. How much harder would it be for someone who doesn't have friends like that?

I don't think that kids who have friends that are working on themselves know how important a role they play.

Shevi

I was in the mall on Sunday with two other kids, and a man comes up behind us, and says to the lady he was with, "Oh no, the Jews are here." So my friends were annoyed at first, and they were getting all defensive, and saying these things about how frustrating it is to always stick out and stuff, and I'm like, "Hey, just a minute. Obviously we stick out! That's a good thing! I'm on G-d's team and I'm wearing His uniform." What's there to be embarrassed of? I LOVE my team colors!

Ellie

You know, I'm sitting down to write in here, and not that I mind doing the journal thing at all, but really, life's not as intense as it ends up coming out on paper. I mean, everything I write is true, but it just ends up sounding way more dramatic than it really is. Just letting you know.

Sarah

Something I've been noticing lately — it used to be that a certain look was "cool." The short jean skirt and tight Hollister/Abercrombie/ American Eagle shirt. But now I look around and see kids dressed like that and I don't find it exceptionally cool or pretty. Maybe the labels still attract my attention, but the way they actually look means more to me now. Now that I shop differently, the same things just aren't cool anymore.

I wonder why so many kids just follow along, trying to hit someone else's standards of what cool is. Why let someone else decide where you shop and dress? Once we started these meetings, and I started learning and working on *tznius*, cool began to mean something totally different. Now, cool is what I make it. If I wanna wear tights every day, I'll pull them on and make that cool. Whatever I decide to wear, I'll do it with confidence and self-assurance — that's cool. If I think it's weird to have a company name scrawled across my front, I'll no longer look at a room full of girls and pick out the "cool" ones by who's wearing those shirts.

But wait. Isn't that judgmental? I'm confused. Isn't that a little bit wrong?

• • •

♥ Avigail

Friday, I went to get a manicure and a pedicure, not something I usually do, but I was in the mood, whatever. So I go in my flip-flops, because my mother dropped me off right in front of the store, and planned on picking me up there, and besides, what else do you wear for a pedicure? It was absolutely shmoiling outside — like the air looked blurry in front of you type of hot, and the place was absolutely *packed* with *frum* ladies.

And you know what? There was a lady next to me getting a pedicure who just took off her tights and stayed till her toes were dry so she could *put them right back on again*. I promise, I never would have even thought of that. It just goes to show that there really is no such thing as the thought, *well, now I have no choice, I just have to...* There's always a choice. There's always an alternative. Cool.

☆ Chavi

I really do not want to be writing in this journal right now. I've been slipping up so much lately that I don't even think you can call it slipping anymore. It's more like doing three backward somersaults and then landing headfirst in a pile of garbage.

So, among all of the changes that I've been making, a few I don't know, months ago I guess, I stopped talking to boys. I mean, no official ignoring announcement went on, but everybody knew about it. And sometimes they still IM or text me and stuff, but I just ignore it. Well, till yesterday, anyway. I still have no idea why I answered, I was just in kind of an uchy mood, and I ended up texting back and forth with him all day. We didn't even talk about anything. As a matter of fact, the only thing we were really saying was that I *don't* talk to boys anymore. Then, finally, I just said, sorry, I really can't do this, and stopped.

Then, like two hours later, I get a text from a different boy (word gets out fast). And I'm like, well, I already broke my rule, might as well talk to this one (who I like better anyway). So he's telling me all about how he heard I flipped, and I'm like, who said that and on and on. So finally he's like, okay, I know you won't hang or anything, but you text, right?

That was my chance to say no. To stand up for what I believe in, to make a point and show that these changes aren't just surface...but I didn't. I just said, "Mmhmm," and "Later Gater." Which led to the whole day of texting today. AAAHHH!

Once you're caught in the fun it's so impossibly hard to stop and do a value check to see if what you're doing is right. I like talking to boys, I really, really do. That would be an embarrassing thing to say, but I know there's not a girl out there who doesn't feel the same way. When I gave up guy friends, I felt like I instantly cut down my social life by more than half. I was suddenly a lot less popular — less phone calls, texts, and all that.

I texted him that I made a mistake, and we really had to stop. I really did mean it this time. Maybe this entry will be the closure that I need to really end these relationships. Not that I think I will stop wanting to have what to do with guys (I don't think that's gonna happen any time soon), but I know that I can't go down that route for my own spiritual health. I don't really think there is a girl who can say she isn't affected religiously by being friends with guys. Unless, of course, they're lying to themselves (something kids are good at).

 Rachel

It's only a couple of weeks till Pesach, and I was walking down the street with my aunt to buy a Haggadah. She's visiting from L.A., and is spending the first days of *yom tov* with us. As we were walking, we bumped into my good friend and her sister. As I was making the introductions, I noticed that my friend was looking at my aunt a little strangely — and then I noticed why. My aunt was wearing pants. I was so used to it on her, I didn't even notice it. I started getting SO annoyed. Like, that is not cool. Don't judge my aunt; you have no idea what she's been through. Don't you dare look at her like that... You're no better than her.

Shevi

This past meeting was a little intense for me. I know that girls don't think of me this way, and I know myself that I'm not the type, and it's not something that I'm proud of...

Okay, start over. I have a boyfriend. I mean, had. He's the brother of a good friend of mine, and it started out that we were just friendly, and then we just got closer, and we started talking on the phone a lot, and I don't know, it just took on a life of its own. We started arguing a lot at the beginning of this year, and now it's one of those long, painful, drawn-out things. I can't tell you how badly I wish I would have stopped this from day one. It's just such a stupid situation, because

I'm SO not like this, but for some reason when it comes to him, I'm like, incapable of logical thinking. It's like, we don't talk for a couple of weeks, then I call him because I'm in a bad mood, then we start thinking about how much we've missed hanging together, so we start, then we realize we shouldn't be talking, so we go back to step one. And if that sounds like fun, let me be clear — it's not. Sometimes I wonder how much this relationship is pulling me down. Like, how much mental and emotional energy is it zapping from my life — and it does. Who would I/could be without him always around me?

Right now we're not speaking, which is good for me, and I can't help but hope that this time it's for real. I just find it funny (well, sad really) when girls handle these relationships so casually, like, "Oh yeah, no big deal, we're just friends," or "So, there will be guys around, but I'm not really gonna talk to any." Like, why are they so sure of themselves? If any girl had to choose the most *tznius* girls in her grade, I think I might get on that list. I'm not saying that to brag, it's just that *tznius* is something that's naturally so, so important to me, I've been super vigilant with the way I dress even before I was a part of this, and it's an area in which I can pretty confidently say I'm strong in. Except for this one part of it: boys. So what makes them think it's any different for them? I think that there is a special *yetzer hara* around these types of issues that makes it exceptionally hard for girls and guys to think clearly. So why put yourself in a position where it's hard for you? Let Hashem take care of testing you, there's no reason to put yourself in a place where you're testing yourself.

♪ Ellie

So tonight after our little boy talk, I went out for pizza. For some reason, the place was *packed* with girls and guys I know, and I just shut down. You know how you were describing it, like turning yourself off, and just observing...it was great. It was like seeing distant relatives I barely know.

They said: "Hi, how are you?"

I said: "Good, and you?"

Them: "Good."

Me: "Good, good, see ya."

Or something like that. I was just how I was supposed to be — finally, after months of frustration and of trying to find the right balance and not letting it be awkward and all that garbage. Just another example of efforts not going to waste.

The first time I wore a completely *tzanua* shirt on a BOILING hot day, I almost cried. I was used to my Hanes, and not caring, and just airy and so, so much simpler, and finally I'm trying to do the right thing and He decides the moment's perfect for a heat wave?! I was so disappointed and uncomfortable. But you know — for the rest of that summer, in those shirts in the heat, whenever my mind would switch into resentment mode, it would quickly snap back — remembering the heat wave and how much worse it could be and thank G-d that's over. And somehow, the day then seemed a lot cooler, and I was a lot more comfortable than I had been five seconds earlier. That gross heat wave right at the beginning of the summer ended up being a *berachah*!

Yeah, I've messed up a lot. I used to spend a lot of my free time with guys, and that stinks for so many reasons. But now, I can refer back to it, relate to other people, understand people's *nisyonos* better, and not resent having to act subdued around boys. A very prolonged and annoying *berachah*, maybe, but a *berachah* nonetheless. And I'm thankful for it. All situations I've been in are for a reason — whether or not I understand it at the time, and I'm thankful for them.

Sarah

The other day my parents were cleaning out a dresser in their room where they keep their important documents like our passports and old report cards and stuff. I looked in while they were in the middle of the process and saw a shirt on my father's bed — my shirt. It's an American Eagle, from eighth grade. Off-white, with AE written in some different material across the front of it. My mother always hated that shirt. I've had worse, I think, but she always had it in for that one. For the past couple of years there were a bunch of times when the laundry would get done and my mother would put my stuff on my bed, but I wouldn't be able to find that shirt because she would "forget" to give it back to me, so I would trek down to the laundry room to get it myself. I guess at some point I just lost track of it. I kinda forgot to look for it. And now, here it was.

"Didn't we give that shirt away?" I really thought we had, as we gave a lot of my stuff away. "No," my mom said, "we're going to burn this one."

I caught her eye and realized she was joking. It's weird to be agreeing with her on these things.

• • •

♥ Avigail

On *chol hamo'ed* Pesach, I had my cousin's bar mitzvah. There were a few older teenage guys there, some random family friends I guess, and the whole night they kept trying to make eye contact and talk to me. It made me so nervous — I kept double-checking to make sure my dress was appropriate, my hair and makeup weren't over the top, I wasn't sending out any signals... Why should they keep bothering me?

I was talking it over with a friend, and she said that after a certain point, when you know that you're as *tznius* as you can be, boys will still be boys. You can — and should — do what you should do, but after a certain point, there's no need to make yourself crazy with guilt if a guy keeps staring at you. As long as you are 100% sure you're not encouraging it, you're not doing anything wrong. He's just being rude. As guys tend to be.

☆ Chavi

This morning that boy texted me again: *Hey girl who doesn't text me anymore.* I shut him down so fast he didn't know what hit him. It was awesome. I would guess that's the last I'll hear from him.

Since I made the decision to stop talking to/hanging out with boys, I've been trying to avoid them at all costs, not wanting to see their reactions. I don't think they're going to understand, let alone respect me for it.

But I had to do it, so I did. It's like every other decision that I've made so far, every other step I've taken to improve my *tznius*, inside and out. It's scary at first. At first, I was just talking about these things because everyone at the meeting was, but I realized how little I need these relationships in my life, and how they aren't good for me and my spiritual growth, for my *neshamah*...for everything we've been learning and speaking about. It just didn't make sense, so I sat down and made a list of pros and cons, and the pros won.

I thought about how some of my friendships would change, and how my schedule, and even my routines would be different from now on — even my contacts list would shrink by fifty percent! But then I thought about how things would change for me, how I would just be able to focus on the things that mean the most, how my life would look afterwards...it's no contest.

Sometimes I wonder what would have been if you hadn't asked me to be part of this group.

❀ Rachel

So I was in my kitchen grating potatoes for Pesach, and I was wearing this ordinary, striped, button-down shirt. My grandmother was in the room with me and my sister, and suddenly she touches my back and says, "Rachel, you really look good in this shirt. It accentuates your waistline." I stared for a second, and then I went into freak-out mode. *What? This shirt accentuates my body? Hold this potato for a minute while I go change!*

I don't get it. It wasn't tight on me or anything; it was just a regular Gap shirt. Was that supposed to be a compliment or constructive criticism? I think she was just trying to be nice. Now that I'm writing this, it's kind of funny.

Shevi

Omgsh, Six Flags on *chol hamo'ed* could be like a *tznius* laboratory, watching everyone and how they act with their friends. It was so sad, because I met so many people I know there, and like everybody was hyper-focused on what everybody was wearing, and how hyper they all were. Uch.

Ellie

So, over Shabbos, I was in a town with lots of used-to-be friends and current friends. I never really hang out at any of their houses so much, because of the whole "scene" and whatever... So, I go to shul and immediately see a bunch of kids I know, and they see me, so I put on my usual "I'm going somewhere *really* important, have no time to talk" face and I rush past with a quick "g'Shabbos." I went into the actual shul, and I see more friends, and I'm wondering how on earth I'm supposed to deal with this scene — it's gonna be really awkward because I used to hang out with all these people!! So, after *davening* I saw them all standing a little sketchily together in a big huddle, and all of a sudden I BURST out laughing and I couldn't stop! Of course, they all thought I was laughing at them, and they got this really annoyed look on their faces, and my friend who was with me thought I was NUTS, and kept telling me to stop laughing, but I couldn't! You know why? Because all of a sudden, they just looked absolutely hilarious!

Think about this for a minute — you get all dressed up and think you're really cool, then go find specific friends to be with while you "casually" walk by other specific friends, then very carefully stop to chat, all the while "casually" flinging your hair over your shoulder, wondering if you still look okay. And if another cool group passes you by, you either end up feeling less cool or try desperately to "casually" join them, so you can stay looking cool yourself. Meanwhile, you're working so hard to keep the whole "I don't really care about any of this, I'm just chilling" look. Once you're out of the scene, it all looks so unbelievably idiotic, you can't help but crack up.

In the beginning, I used to wish that it was different — that I could still hang out, and have fun with the guys, and feel all cool like that. But time passed and my whole life just runs differently, and it's become hard not to pity the kids still trapped in the scene.

The pressure's off — I can stay home and play dumb board games with my sisters, lay around on the couch talking to my mother, not see a single boy, and still feel cool enough to tell anyone in the world that that's exactly how I spent my weekend. Kids may think it's easier to make these types of changes after seminary — that's classic — and they see it as the easier way out, and still end up fine. Well, I guess if you consider the easy way out dancing in circles, pressuring others and themselves into thinking that that's the cool thing to do, and constantly stressing over the drama of the whole thing — well, that's a little ridiculous, don'tcha think?

 **Sarah**

Pesach ended up being really annoying. I made up some stupid excuse to avoid going to Six Flags — I just wanted to avoid the whole scene. I tried to forget that my closest friend just told me that she has a boyfriend, while I just decided to stop talking to boys, and I tried to block out all the teasing of the kids who keep calling me a nerd just because they miss me.

Why should I care about them anyway? This is about ME this time. This is the only time in my life that I allow myself to be totally selfish — when the only other option is not *being* myself. It's funny that each and every change that I've worked so hard to incorporate into my life over the past year is probably just a huge blur to them, just lumped under the category of me "flipping out."

Sometimes someone compliments me on something I'm wearing, and that's huge. Compliments were never really a big deal to me, but when you're still walking that tightrope of whether or not to dress a certain way, that one compliment can make such an enormous difference.

I'm just trying not to let anything throw me off. To keep my eyes on the prize, on the goal — whether it's not wearing clothes that are too tight today, or not saying certain words tomorrow, or not watching a certain movie the next day. I'll do it. I have to.

MAY

What Are We Afraid Of?

THE EIGHTH MEETING

When I posed the family question at the eighth meeting, the answers were very different — and heartening.

When I say "*tznius*," what comes to mind?

- Confident
- Modest
- G-dly
- Beautiful
- Separate
- Internality

What stops us from being *tznius*?

The answers seem obvious, but the *yetzer hara* is endlessly creative. Among other rationalizations:

- My mother likes it when I dress this way.
- Everyone wears it so it must be okay.
- The halachah isn't clear on this issue.
- I'll only wear it around my house.
- I don't want to look like a nerd.
- When I lose weight it will fit better.
- I won't sit down.
- I won't raise my arm.
- I like the way I look like this.
- It's just too hard.

As Rabbi Eliezer Stern said in a speech given to his students at Prospect Park High School, it's a smokescreen. The *yetzer hara* is attacking our most precious gift.

We went through the excuses one by one to rip them apart, but the point wasn't to refute these specific reasons, because tomorrow there will be another convincing one to add to the list. The point was to recognize the fact that the *nisayon* is strong. Catching yourself rationalizing is a large part of fighting the battle.

As for the last excuse, that *tznius* is just too hard — is it? Yes, of course it is a very hard mitzvah to keep, but if we are constantly having to force ourselves to meet the requirements of halachah, if the whole thing seems like such a huge burden and the other look is so overwhelmingly tempting, then something is deeply off in our understanding of *tznius*. On some level, we need to investigate what *tznius* means in a deeper way, and find out exactly where our challenges are stemming from.

That said, it is a difficult thing to maintain a constant awareness of the letter and the spirit of the law. But there are things we can do to make it easier.

Firstly, I told them to beware the "drop one, drop all syndrome." It's something everyone does when on a diet: you slip once and cheat a little during the day, and then before you know it, it's, "oh well, I already blew it, I may as well eat that pint of ice cream." The same holds true in the spiritual world. When we slip up, as we inevitably will, we have a tendency to think that we blew it, so what's the point of continuing to try. This attitude is a farce. We're not expected to be perfect, we're expected to keep working.

We can also harness the power of a group. If peer pressure is a huge force for the negative, it is equally as strong for the positive, and working on something together with a group of like-minded people is an enormously effective technique.

Make it easier for yourself: Don't buy the clothes! Don't keep them in your closet! Don't shop in certain stores! Don't hang out with those kids! *Tznius* is difficult enough without the things that we are constantly doing to sabotage ourselves.

And the last tip — recognize its importance, appreciate its beauty, learn about its benefits. And make peace with the fact that you're going to need to be constantly vigilant to protect your standards.

We ended off by discussing another tactic of the *satan*. We look around, and we're pretty comfortable where we are holding. We may not be the *frummest* in our neighborhood, but let's face it, we never will be. We're certainly not the worst, either, so we're right in the middle of the road. We're the ones that are always "just right." So we feel okay.

Hashem doesn't judge like that. You aren't evaluated sideways, in comparison with those around you, you're compared up and down — how far you've come from where you started. You don't get *schar* for the things you've been programmed to do — those aren't your battles, it's too easy. You get rewarded for how you grew. It's not enough to maintain the status quo because you're comfortable there. It's all about how hard we push ourselves.

• • •

♡ Avigail

Okay, you're not going to believe this story, *I* wouldn't even believe this story if I wouldn't know for a fact that it was 100% true. Which I do, because it happened to me. Here it is:

My sister was driving me home from a friend's house and she had on this awful CD in the car — I don't know what it was, but it was really getting on my nerves. Well, I know she doesn't listen to English music, but I was in one of those lousy, I really don't care type of moods, so I switched on the radio, something I haven't done in a *long* time, and for some reason, she just let me keep it on. So the music's filling up the car, and I'm just feeling vaguely guilty because it's been so long since I listened to this type of music, and while there was nothing really wrong with the song that was playing...I don't know. So I start asking my sister things like, "What's up with the whole music thing, like, is it really that big of a deal to listen to music like this, and is it true that the lyrics can fall under *tznius*... Is it really that important to only listen to Jewish stuff..." and all those types of questions, and as all these things are going through my head, all of a sudden my sister says, "Avigail, look in front of us." So I did. And there is a shiny black car with a man at the wheel.

And his license plate reads: JMUSIC.

☆ Chavi

Did you ever see something that's totally out of place and think, okay, that's weird, but at the same time it's just so normal? Let me help you if I'm being super vague right now. I was on a bus last night on my way back home, and I'm sitting in the window seat, and we pass a baseball team playing on a diamond. The field had these super bright lights beaming on the people and it really looked like for that team, it was smack in middle of the day! It was night everywhere except for where they were playing. A patch of daytime really doesn't belong in the night, and yet, there it was. It was as if they could stretch out the day to be as long as they wanted because they had those lights, blocking out what the rest of the world was doing. I thought that was really cool. It just goes to show that it is possible to block out the night that's all around us, and we don't have to accept it.

Okay, I know that's really cheesy, but really, if someone hands you those lights and you get a handyman electricity person to wire them up, and the *only* thing you have to do is flip the switch, would you? It's scary and it's hard — and if you're thinking, "Well, how hard could it be to flip a switch?" — I'll tell you: extremely hard. You see, if you're sitting in the dark, thinking about turning the switch, and there are pressures not to from home, school, everywhere around you, then you just can't seem to make sense of anything. After all, it's hard to think in the dark. And even if you manage to flick on the light, they should really come with a warning label thing, because these lights often get tripped, and then you're back to the exact same place of needing to flick the switch again. So there are those people who give up before even trying, and they try to make it look cool to not even bother, and they convince other people to do the same: "Chill out! The dark's fun!" But can you imagine if *everybody* would turn on their lights, then there would be no dark, and no pressure to stay there?! We could stretch the day into infinity. That would be something.

Rachel

I think that *tznius* on the inside is so much harder to work on than *tznius* on the outside, at least for me. I'm probably just saying that because that's what I'm focused on right now, but it just seems harder to pin down. It's not as obvious as changing your shirt. Then, at least, there's some recognition, some reaction from people. You can walk away feeling like something was done. But when I stop myself from hogging the spotlight or looking at something inappropriate, no one knows about it but me and Hashem. No one is commenting because it's not apparent. Maybe that's why it's so much harder. I'm so used to the strong reactions I got from changing the way I dress externally, that I don't know where to go without them. I have less motivation, and that scares me. Why do I rely on the reactions of others so much? And how can I motivate myself to change on the inside even though other people can't see it?

Shevi

I went home with a friend last night, and I sat on a bus that had girls and boys on it. Anyways, there was this kid in my class who I started to talk to after I sat down, and when we pulled up to the stop that the boys got on she suddenly stopped. She never picked up our conversation, and then a few minutes after we pulled off, she sent me a text apologizing, saying how she really tries hard not to call attention to herself. So every single day she plugs in her iPod, and just becomes the silent one for the rest of the trip.

She's been doing this every day for a year. It's unbelievable.

Ellie

School is kind of an illusion. Our dress code's not that specific, so people still look normal and it's easy to believe that they dress like that outside of school, too. Recently I bumped into three girls walking together in the city. They were dressed *totally* not like in school, and it's funny because they actually brought up the fact that they were so happy to finally get to wear their non-school clothes because it was nice weather, and they wouldn't be bumping into teachers or anything. I was (stupidly) really shocked at what I saw and heard, because while I'm really close with these girls, I kinda had assumed they were the type to treat themselves better than that.

School is constantly reminding us that just because we may have vacation from classes, *halachos* don't stop applying. Just because we have to follow them in school, doesn't make them school rules. I thought that the message was getting kind of old, but I guess I was only thinking of myself... (What else is new.)

And who's to say it stops at clothes! Just because they give us *davening* time in school, should we take Sundays to relax and say, "Oh, thank G-d it's Sunday, now I don't have to daven"?!

People who act like that have their reasons, I guess, but nobody actually thinks it's okay. We have a kosher snack machine in school, but no one stuffs their face with McDonalds on Sundays because there's no school...because it's STILL WRONG.

So why should *tznius* be any different? If anything, it should be more important outside of school, not less. Why should a kid say to me, "Uch Ellie, don't worry. It's Sunday, no one's gonna see."

I hate to break it to you hun, He's gonna see.

Sarah

So, Wednesday night I go with my dad to Target. Best store ever. (Didn't I say that about H & M? Oh well.) Wait, let me just start by saying that I hate shopping with him. First of all, he hates shopping, so he has absolutely no patience. Also, he's totally paranoid about every article of clothing. Like, he doesn't know whether or not to trust me that they're okay. He can't tell by just looking at the skirt or sweater or whatever, so everything I take off the rack, practically everything I touch, he'll be like — wait, would Mommy approve of this? Insanely annoying.

Anyway, the best was Wednesday night. So we're in the store, and I'm trying on a skirt and a sweater. The skirt is fine, totally past the knees, perfect. The sweater is a size small, but it looks too big on me. I don't mean big as in not snug, I mean big as in unattractively falling-off-the-shoulders big. As in, I need an extra-small type big. So I'm standing in front of the mirror, turning this way and that, and I'm thinking, can I wear this? Like, is it really big, or am I just used to tighter stuff? So I decide to go out and get the extra-small to compare. I come out of the dressing room all proud of at least comparing the two, and not just automatically reaching for the smaller one like I used to, and I meanwhile hand my father the skirt. "Would this be okay with Mommy?" he says. My fists clenched, I answer, "Yeah, it's totally fine, don't worry." He still looks doubtful, and then he gestures to the sweater. "Okay...and what's with the sweater?"

"Well, it's kinda big, I just wanted to try an extra-small."

"No, an extra-small is gonna be too small."

I'm starting to clench my fists again. "But even Mommy —"

He interrupts me. "No buts. Do you want the size small or not?"

So I think about it for a second. Maybe it doesn't look that bad, I think, and even so, there's always the dryer... So I say, "Yeah," and I'm trying not to make a big deal about it. But inside, I'm like, *Hashem, what do you want from me already? I'm trying so hard, but every time I feel like I've come so far, I get zero encouragement! My parents don't acknowledge my effort, my friends couldn't care less...where are You in all this?*

Would Mommy approve? Who CARES?! It wasn't her decision to work on *tznius*, it was MINE! She doesn't deserve any credit — why should she get the satisfaction of thinking that I only wear what she approves of? This just isn't her game to play anymore. It's all me now. Me and G-d and that's all.

Of course I want to make my mother proud. But has she said anything about how I started wearing tights everyday? Or about how I got rid of my tight shirts, or three of my favorite skirts because they were too short? No, she didn't! She never said, "Wow, Sarah, I'm so proud of you!" or anything like that! So why should she suddenly get down my back about the clothing that I want to buy? That's not how it works. I'm not saying that I don't think she's proud of me. It could be that she's suffocating in *nachas* and joy and blah, blah, blah. But why not say anything to let me know she cares?!

So I ranted and raved for a while in the car about this, and you know what my father said? He said that the reason why they haven't said anything about all of the changes I've been making in *tznius*, is because they don't know how I'll respond. They think I would rather they not acknowledge it at all.

Well, I'm not really sure how that miscommunication happened, but whatever.

So I come home, and my mother's like, "Hey, let's see what you got!" She always does that, like not to make it obvious that she really just wants to make sure the *tznius* is up to par. So I patiently show her everything, and she gets up to the skirt and holds it up. "Is this long enough?"

"Yes," I said through my teeth.

She holds up the sweater. "It's cute! What size is it?" My frustration is mounting now.

"Small."

"And it's not too tight?"

I almost want to laugh. "No, it's not too tight, Mommy, don't worry."

Maybe eventually she'll tell me she's proud of me. Maybe my father will tell her what I said, and they'll acknowledge how hard I've been working, and maybe they'll both learn how to trust my judgment.

Okay, enough parent bashing. You should know that my parents rock ninety percent of the time, and I love them like crazy.

• • •

♥ Avigail

Wore tiny socks and Crocs today instead of tights, because I thought we were going on a class trip, but it was cancelled. I passed by Mrs. X in the hallway, and literally turned PURPLE. I don't think she even saw my legs, I don't even think she could care less, but I was sooo embarrassed. What is this group doing to me?!

☆ Chavi

It's way past midnight now, and I really need to get to sleep, but I just want to write about something that happened this morning. I was on the bus going to school and I hear these two girls kinda fighting with each other. Usually I have my iPod on to the loudest volume and I don't hear anything except for, well, my music, but this morning I needed to review for my *Navi* test. Anyway, listening to these two girls was great. One was telling the other — wait, I'll make this easier to follow — A tells B that she's not gonna cover her knees, elbows etc, unless she understands why she's doing it. When I heard that, I thought about what I would have added to the argument six months ago. I would have said the same thing — don't do things you don't understand. B was saying how she's learning so much from a certain older girl and she's taking baby steps... Omgsh, I can not tell you how heated this argument between them got. You also have no idea how much I felt badly for A, because she was so missing out. It's a certain stage, and I know it too well, when you think you have all the answers, because for the most part you're arguing with people who don't know their stuff. I wanted to scream that she's totally missing the point, the potential, the everything. But I didn't. I wanted to help her. I wanted to let her in on the secret.

But it would have been weird to mix in, so I didn't. Too bad. The fight continued on to judging people, and then the feeling of what's the point if there's so much to do...and on and on and on. It's not every day you get to hear something like this. It was like listening to my past. Lol.

❀ Rachel

Okay, so I have this friend. A really, really close friend who I've been going to school with forever. She's definitely not the same as me, but we talk about everything together. She's an amazing girl, but she just tends to get influenced easily by other people. That said, I was still really surprised by something that happened the other day.

She was coming over to spend the day at my house, studying. I was wearing my usual type outfit, whatever it was that day, and she came in wearing one of those V-neck Hanes tee-shirts, which are SO not okay to wear alone on *anyone*. It came so low that I had to look away — it was embarrassing. I was so, so...surprised, I guess. I mean, it was upsetting to me in general that she thought it was okay to wear something like that around me, and also...I just couldn't understand. I was so taken aback that I couldn't comment. Besides, what would I have said? I don't want people to think of me as the *tznius* police.

But sometimes I really think I should say something. Like, I'm being a bad friend by pretending that these things don't matter. But I don't want to come off sounding rude or mean. I had so many openings with this girl that day, but I just avoided them. It was almost as if she *wanted* me to say something, that's how many times she sort of brought it up. And now she probably thinks that I think there's nothing wrong with it. I just don't get it — how could she think that shirt is okay? I wish I had said something. I really do care about her. I wish I had said something.

Shevi

So today I went shopping and was looking for a skirt. I got a cute one, but I was in a rush, and didn't really check it out well. So I get home, try it on for my sister, and...yup. Too tight. It's so annoying because it's the perfect length and color and everything else! So it's sitting on my bed, right next to me as I write this, waiting for me to make my decision. I know I should return it, but...I don't want to.

I guess I'll wait till tomorrow to decide.

♪ Ellie

I took over my friend's lifeguarding for the day, and I'm sitting in this huge room by the empty pool. Women's swim is not till eight, so I'm in long sleeves and a skirt until then. I'm hoping no men drown before that.

The scary man who comes to check the pool just came in.

Him: You ready to jump in and save someone in that outfit?

Me: Yup.

Him: It won't slow you down in case of an emergency?

Me: Um...there's no one in the pool.

Him: But if there was, you would take all that clothing off?

Me: Um...well, no.

Then he left. Lol.

Sarah

After a week-long *tznius* class by one of my teachers, one of my friends texted me last night: "Something really weird happened. I went to the mall and everything was too short or just not good it's really weird."

I love her. I wanted to tell her that it's not weird, she was just recognizing her *bushah* — it's just *tznius*. But I didn't. Anyway, later she told me that she needs to go shopping because she just isn't comfortable with a lot of her clothing.

I don't know what made me feel better — knowing that she's changing and watching what I must have looked like a few months ago, or realizing that she feels comfortable telling me this stuff and talking to me about *tznius*/growing because she knows I'll respect her. Either way, it made me feel really good.

• • •

♡ Avigail

I was thinking recently about something you asked us at the first meeting: How high does *tznius* rate in our *avodas Hashem*? I originally said like a four. I'm now definitely at a *ten*. Why? Not because I'm dressed differently, not because I threw out bag after bag of clothing. But because I'm *thinking* differently. I just find myself thinking about my place in this physical world differently from the way I did before I focused on the concept of *tznius*. I realize that I was created for a dual purpose: (1) to serve Hashem, like to daven to Him, trust Him, praise Him, thank Him, do His mitzvos; and (2) to emulate Him — to walk around and be a constant reminder to the world of His existence. When I'm dressed like everyone else, or even like every average teenager, I'm not making any statements — I'm just blending in. But when I dress, talk, and act in a *tznius* and *frum* (and still normal) way, then there's a message on my shirt and skirt and tights. The message says, "I'm a Jew, and I'm cool like that."

✫ Chavi

When I wake up in the morning, it's just become this routine to go straight to the *tznius* clothing — no joke. I mean no, that's not completely true. It's not *just* a routine — it's a special routine that I'm so happy I do — I just don't want to forget why I'm doing it. So I think, and I say, okay I'm wearing this...

Because it's the right thing to do.

Because I'm proud to be wearing the uniform.

Because I'm not a blind follower.

Because *tznius* means a lot to me.

Because I *want* to.

Rachel

You know how we were talking about getting used to something like covering your legs or wearing looser shirts, and then you feel funny *not* wearing those sort of those things? So there is this girl who lives in California and we're friends and stuff, and something that we *used* to have in common is music; we had very similar taste. So anyway, she emailed me this song that she said I would like, and I start listening, and soon — very soon — I start getting extremely uncomfortable. I mean, I know I'm not Miss Righteous when it comes to music, but yeah, it was weird. *So* not ok. Of course, I never heard the song before, so it wasn't like I knew what was coming.

I was so ewed (I call it the "ew effect.") The ew effect is actually good for you sometimes. It reinforces my negative feelings towards TV and stupid music. I do feel left out in the TV sense sometimes, like when people ask me If I saw last night's episode of the new dance show or something, and then go, "Oops, I forgot you don't watch anymore!" So yeah, sometimes...but I know it's not really good for me and my thoughts — and that's way more important to me then feeling included in some waste-of-time TV drama.

Shevi

I don't think that weather affects me so much in *tznius* clothing wise. I taught myself that it's not so hard to be *tznius* in the summer, because that's when the real test is. Obviously, in the winter it's easier to cover up, because it's cold and everyone does it. I kind of look forward to the heat of the summer, when I can really show what I believe in, *tznius*-wise. That's when I take my stand.

♪ Ellie

I forgot to change before my game tonight. I needed to take off my tights and put on pants, then take off one skirt and put on another, replace tights with socks, all in middle of a wide-open field! The team was supposed to be practicing, but seeing my dilemma they quickly came and made a full circle around me and stayed like that for as long as it took for me to change.

1. I don't know how I would have pulled that off without them.

2. They changed it from something annoying that they had to do into something absolutely hysterical, and everyone was cracking up.

3. Realistically, my team could have totally laughed at me, or asked why I cared so much about being in pants for two seconds.

Just goes to show that *tznius* really doesn't have to be a burden at all, with the right outlook. When I'm surrounded by friends and teammates, who are all dressed in skirts and long sleeves, it's a lot easier to feel proud and love how we look.

Sarah

Another thing that I've been struggling with is what to wear to ball practice. No one on our team or our coach cares what we wear — pants, shorts, short sleeves, skirts, whatever. The hard part really is the shirts. You have no idea how hot — and annoying — it gets to play a sport in long sleeves. The most annoying thing of all is that no one cares either way and I don't *have* to do anything. I'm not gonna lie, it's a constant struggle. I'll update you on that.

• • •

♥ Avigail

Are you ready for this one? The school doesn't let me run for G.O. because of *tznius* VIOLATIONS!!!

At first I was really upset. Then I cracked up.

I was upset because after all the work I've done on myself, my earlier self is still coming back to haunt me. Then I laughed because it showed me how far I'd come.

Oh well.

☆ Chavi

So, if you keep asking Dave for those green shakes after he makes white, I guarantee he'll get the point. You'll be that customer who he'll point at and ask, "The usual?"

I went to my friend's house tonight, and she goes home on a co-ed bus. So this one boy walks up to me, and he's like, "Haven't seen you in forever blah, blah, blah." I almost ran the other way. Anyhow, this was when I didn't just talk the talk, I walked the walk. I put my ideas and beliefs into action. You just can't be scared or embarrassed to ask Dave to redo your milk shake, because white mint is SO not worth it. I hope to get to the level where I don't even need to ask him cuz he knows; that my skirts will always cover, that I don't talk to boys, that I don't listen to or watch certain stuff. You know, it's good to know when your work is paying off. Because really, you can just get shy and take the white shake, no questions asked — you can get used to the white, no doubt. But why settle when you can have so much more?

 # Rachel

I'm working on not demanding so much attention for myself. Like, letting others speak, and not topping every story. It does not mean I have to be shy or quiet or anything, I just want to watch other kids shine. Not everything has to be about me.

Confession: I have a shirt that I wear that's kind of tight, but whenever I wear it, someone tells me I look skinnier. I'm totally not obsessed with skinniness, but it's still hard not to care.

Shevi

Listen to this: this weekend my ex asked me to hang out, and I looked at him, laughed, and gave such a confident no, it was awesome. It was the first time that I was able to say no and feel good about it

Ellie

Even though it's uplifting and I feel good about it while making decisions in *tznius*, it doesn't mean that the feelings last every time I'm inconvenienced by all the rules. I know we are supposed to be princesses, but sometimes I don't want to be a princess. I just want to be a teenage girl. I don't regret making the decisions that I made — it's just really hard to keep up a positive attitude throughout. But that's really ok, because the whole point is not for it to be easy, it's to effect change. To dress and act in a certain way wasn't a decision I made to make my life easier. It's just something that was right! Does this make sense? I don't have to say, "I love dressing like a nun in 90-degree weather," because that wouldn't be real. It's supposed to be a challenge, so as long as I'm up for that challenge, I'm getting somewhere.

Sarah

Tightness is something that is really hard for me. Let me make this clear — wearing something tight makes me feel uncomfortable because I *know* it's tight. My issue is more when I'm wearing something that's not at all tight, and I always just feel like it looks bad on me. I just sort of feel like it makes me look...ich.

Sometime though, it's not hard at all.

Actually...k, I'm thinking...nope. That's a lie. Wearing not tight stuff is not so hard. What's hard is those in-between shirts. The ones that are probably kind of tight, just not sooo obviously tight that my standards would say they're illegal. So maybe I need to up my standards? I'm not sure about this.

JUNE

Diving In

THE LAST MEETING

Rabbi Twersky speaks about the two things that Yisro heard, which convinced him to join the Jewish people: *kerias Yam Suf* and the war against Amalek. These two incidents can represent the two ways a Jew works on himself while traveling the path of the Torah.

Kerias Yam Suf represents our ability to jump in, to take the plunge. It shows our capacity to disregard our past and submerge ourselves in a new mitzvah, in a new life.

The war with Amalek symbolizes all the things that try to cool us off and lessen our initial enthusiasm. It's the true fight that begins after the first flash of eagerness wears off.

Combined, the ability to jump in and fight our way through any given *nisayon* will ensure our success in every area of our *avodas Hashem*.

The first couple of months into this project the girls were really enthusiastic. They were excited about being chosen, and they were ready to listen and reflect. Newness tends to wear off quickly, and the true battle began after they made peace with the ideas and began to actually put them into practice in their lives. Their journals reflect their successes (and some of their failures) better than anything else. I was consistently impressed and inspired with the honesty of their intro-spection and the strength of their convictions. I think of them, and then think back to what I was like as a teenager in high school, and I was — and am — overwhelmed.

I am embarrassed to be the one to have put together this book. I am in no way, and don't pretend to think I am, a model of *tznius*. But, *tznius* is something I am aware of and working on in my life. The *zechus* to have spent the year working on all of these concepts with these girls is something I will always be grateful for. In these past ten months, I have understood and internalized concepts in *tznius* more than I have in the past ten years. If *tznius* is an art, then these girls have become artists of the highest caliber. May they continue down the paths they've started with the courage and strength they've shown so far.

● ● ●

♡ Avigail

October, November, December, January, February, March, April, May, June.

Not even nine full months. Wow. I don't know where to start. At the beginning of this year, I guess I was like every other high school kid, but now I feel...luckier. I'm lucky because now that things have been explained to me, I'm not disillusioned like a lot of my friends. I don't think my body is who I am. You know, it's funny, I knew I didn't used to dress with *tznius*, but I was totally fine with it — I actually liked it. All the attention, etc... But, I was never *happy*, because feeling pretty alone can't make you happy. Doing what I know is right despite the pressure, that makes me happy. Knowing that what I'm doing is in my best interests and is good for my *olam hazeh* and *olam haba*, that makes me happy. I can't say that I understand every little detail, but I love the feelings of self-worth and holiness I get with *tznius*.

Before this year, I guess I was just uninformed, or maybe I just didn't care. But not anymore. I believe it is my responsibility to care. *Tznius* is still hard for me, it's a lifelong struggle, but I know that others are in this with me, and that G-d is cheering me on. I feel like I can understand, at least a little, what life is all about. It's about Hashem, it's about *kedushah*, it's about sanctity. And the key to all that is *tznius*.

⭐ Chavi

I used to think that doing and dressing according to my family's standards was good enough. I used to think that a few inches couldn't possibly make a difference. I used to think that the laws were abstract. The land I stand on now is more solid, my foundations are stronger.

I no longer think of *tznius* as a burden, as rules that I keep so I don't get into trouble in school. It's a privilege, a goal I aim to approach each day of my life. Over the past year, I've made a few changes. Longer skirts, longer sleeves, looser shirts...but I don't think the importance is in the listing — I just try to keep halachah to the best of my ability.

When I look at pictures of myself from not even so long ago, I can't get over how I was dressed. It's a weird feeling to be looking at myself doing and wearing things that I would never do or wear now. I just don't understand what I was thinking then. I think that in a way, I just shut myself down. Shut down my head, shut down my heart. No thinking. So, then, how did this group get my attention? Sometimes you can recognize among the pretenders, the fakers, those who can do it. I was a faker, and as far as I can tell I was a pretty good one. So how did you know?

How did you know that all I needed was a little push? That I was sitting at the edge wondering what would happen if I jumped. I know I have not landed yet, my feet are nowhere near the ground, but I'm headed there. To think that I would have still been sitting there at the edge wondering...

🌸 Rachel

This is really weird, because I still remember you taking me into the office at the beginning of the year with all these journals stacked up in your arms. I honestly didn't really understand what you were talking about when you described this whole *tznius* thing. And I was also scared. I didn't really want to make the commitment, but at the same time I felt like it would be so stupid of me to turn down something like this. I mean, there had to be a reason why you chose me, right?

Then I came to the first meeting and, to tell you the truth, sitting around the table with all the girls for the first time was just plain awkward. I never really had much to do with any of the younger kids, and those my age I was definitely friendly with but... So that left me, basically sitting by myself, waiting to see what these meetings actually were.

During the meeting itself, I think I spoke only three words, and only when you asked me to. Sometimes I felt like an imposter, because it seemed like everyone else had meaningful things to say and I just sat there. I really thought everyone was looking at me and wondering why on earth I was there. And then I wondered why on earth I was there.

To tell you the truth, I never really knew that *tznius* was something I still needed to be working on. I mean, I·know that it's never good to stand still and stop growing, but I never thought it necessarily applied to *tznius*. Obviously, I only thought of *tznius* as clothing at that point.

Anyway, so in the end the group became so much more then six random kids and a teacher. Sounds cheesy, I know. Sorry. But what would I have done this year without these girls? If someone would have told me in the beginning of the year that I would be so close to kids so much younger than me, I never would have believed it.

The meetings in general made me feel like I was a part of something big. If there was ever a time when I was unsure of what to wear, I thought of the group. They were my cheerleaders when I put a shirt back on the rack. I was always thinking of the group as my conscience, and it always helped make the better decision. Also, finding out that people looked up to me and noticed how I dressed really affected me a lot. Everything changes when you realize you are a role model and people believe in you.

When you read our journals out loud, every time you got up to my entries, I felt like I couldn't breathe. It felt weird hearing from you what I was writing, and the entire time I just stared at my lap. I mean, it felt good for everyone to know what was going on inside my head, but it was a strange mix of good and scary. I don't know. Weird.

If I had to give a piece of advice to somebody about *tznius*, it would be to draw lines for yourself. Decide what you will and will not do, and stick to it.

Honestly, more than anything else, being a part of this group, gave me clarity — I have been *tznius* for a while, but the question was, why. If every teenager looked at *tznius* the way this group got me to, I think they would all dress differently.

Shevi

This year flew by. I think that, more than anything else, this year changed how I view the concept of *tznius* in general. I mean, *tznius* has always been a part of my life, but that was basically because I was raised like that. Not that it was never hard for me, it was just something that was a given. Hearing everyone else's struggles and thoughts about *tznius* was really inspiring. It felt sort of like we were in a support group — lol.

Something else that this group did for me was change how I always subconsciously thought about *tznius* as something nerdy. I realize that a big part of *tznius* is learning how to be modest *and* beautiful. That's something I'm really, really proud of.

♪ Ellie

I remember what I was wearing that day, the day that marked the end of one time in my life and the beginning of another. It seems a little sad, looking back, that that's the thing I see clearest in my head now; maybe it was because I was so self-conscious of my tight, green Hollister shirt with HCO scrawled across it while I sat there being offered a chance to join this group all about *tznius*. Maybe it's because I'm a 16-year-old girl living in the 21st century and that's what teenage girls are like: we're very external and materialistic people; clothing and looks are our top priorities and, apparently, also what sticks out most in our memories.

I remember the night of the first meeting feeling like a total idiot surrounded by these girls I felt like I barely knew, some of whom I thought were perfect people who couldn't possibly have anything to gain from this group because they were so amazing already. There was nothing inherently the same about any of us. For the most part, we came from different communities, had different friends, different family situations, different upbringings. But the one thing that tied us all together was our desire to learn more about this mitzvah.

As the year progressed, we met more and more, and I learned that we all had a lot more in common than we thought, and together we all discovered ourselves and each other. Many misunderstandings and misconceptions about *tznius* and the laws of *tznius* were explained to us; guidelines were set, challenges were overcome, friendships were formed. But nothing was simple. I remember coming out of the first few meetings feeling down and guilty and horrible about myself. There were times when I was upset at myself for being the way I was, and even more upset for not being able to stand up and make the necessary changes. Change is hard. I've always been afraid of change, and I still am, even through all the transformations I underwent in the last year.

By midyear, the greatest breaking point, I was attached to the group, to the meetings. I loved them, even when the information I learned shocked me, hurt me, or challenged my current lifestyle. It became my lifeline, a part of me. The other girls are my friends now, my mentors, and my role models. We helped each other grow in ways we didn't know was possible, at times when it seemed like nothing was. I realized that none of us was born perfect, or *tzanua*, and that most of us had a very long way to go. Even today, we all still struggle with *tznius* and its laws, because it is a lifelong struggle, but we are all so much further than we ever dreamed we'd be. Some of us threw away or ripped up articles of clothing; others went on shopping trips together and replaced the entire contents of their closets; still more made other crucial changes in their mindsets that you read about (I guess...weird). All of it, though, was for the better.

I remember the first time I decided to wear tights outside of school. I remember putting them on in the morning, feeling like a million dollars for making the right decision, and then feeling like two cents when my friends looked at me funny for it later. My friends eventually got over it, though, and so did I. But tights and longer skirts and looser shirts weren't the main things I got out of these meetings. Looking back, I realize that after all the hardships, the pain, the joy, the challenges, the breakthroughs, the different friendships and wardrobes, I was a new person. I didn't need to pretend to not care about halachah anymore. I didn't need to guiltily pull at my shirts, knowing how tight they were. But most of all, I was no longer afraid to do the right thing. Because, of all the things this group has given me, the most important was this newfound courage — the courage to stand apart.

Sarah

Last journal entry. Insane.

So you asked us how we have changed. That's actually a really hard question to answer, because once you've changed so much internally and externally, it's hard to think back and relate the person you are to the way you used to think or act. I know this though: I like myself better now.

I think that *tznius* is a multifaceted mitzvah. You can't just *do tznius*.

You have to also *be tznius*. Even in the beginning, just the idea of being part of this group meant that I *had* to make some changes. I think the first concrete change was wearing tights, which was really easy in the winter when everyone else was wearing them. But that's really the easiest way to start changing. I don't think there is anything wrong with starting something good because everybody around you is doing it too. The other girls in the group made me realize that you can be really good and really cool at the same time, and that was the biggest influence on me this year.

So when did it stop becoming about *them* and start becoming about *me*? I think with each of these meeting I just started thinking differently — it became more and more apparent that not only were certain things were wrong, but *why*.

Cuz it's low.

Cuz it's gross.

Cuz it looks bad.

Cuz it's not worth it.

Cuz it's just not appropriate.

And slowly that became —

Cuz it's just not *me*.

I worked so hard to get to that point, where wearing or saying certain things was just... uch. So I can definitely say that I am proud of myself.

But before you start your applause, I'll admit that I have a long way to go still, and I always will. There will always be something to improve on, and work on, and grow from — always.

So I am not gonna lie. I am a little scared and nervous for the summer and next year — without these meetings and the journals and everything. I know I'll never revert back to the way I once was, but I don't want to be stuck, either. I don't want to stay this way, I want to keep growing.

So that's it. My last entry. This group changed my life.

Oh — and you guys reading this, one last thing — GOOD LUCK (it's so worth it).

Appendix A
THE LETTERS

Girls —

I realized after our...thing last night that though we spent much time on what a *tzanua* does not look like — shy, wallflower, etc. — we never really clarified what she <u>does</u> look like — and that's really the more important thing.

So: what does a *tzanua* look like? She's confident, beautiful, sure of herself. She is full of Jewish pride, and she doesn't feel the need to flaunt her body. Her "outer" radiates her "inner" and she is very much in touch with her soul.

K, now look in the mirror. Then write about it.

See you in 2 weeks.

Mrs. Goldin

• • •

So, I'm getting the feeling that many of you are disappointed that I haven't written any sort of response or comments in your journals.

I didn't think you would want me to. I sorta figured you would prefer to just pretend I don't look at it at all.

In any case, your journals are awesome. You are awesome. You are doing a perfect job and if there is one piece of advice I can give about the journals — WRITE MORE.

Write all of your thoughts on the topic, look around and comment about what you see, etc. Most importantly — be honest. Try to include your thoughts about anything we spoke about at the meeting.

Have a great Shabbos, girls.

Mrs. Goldin

• • •

Guys,

I'm gonna be out for a bit and I just want to give you some guidelines till we meet again (does next Monday night work for you? Let me know).

Have you ever known anyone whose outside did not match her inside? Can you write about it?

Has there ever been a specific time when your outside didn't match your inside? Can you write about that, too?

And one more thing — if you've ever seen one, can you write about a girl/woman (preferably a girl) who is a *tzanua* and inspires you.

And don't forget to think about what we've talked about, look around, and write some more.

Mrs. Goldin

P.S. Oh, and what is up with the Abercrombie shopping bags?! Do you see anything wrong with them? What about the ones with just guys — anything wrong with those? Why? Why not? Do you have any issues with carrying them around? Just curious.

• • •

Okay guys,

I'm a little overwhelmed by your journals; I'm not really sure where to start. It seems you're finding this project a little bit heavy, particularly the last meeting. With a few exceptions, your latest entries were really...depressing.

And I keep asking myself why I started this whole thing to begin with.

Can I be honest with you guys (being that I'm basically asking you to let me into your heads on this topic, and I know it's been hard and awkward for some of you — the truth is it's only right for me to be somewhat honest myself, I guess) at the risk of depressing you more, the issues that you're having with *tznius* don't get easier as you grow up, though the specifics may change. The truth of the matter is that the despairing feeling at the never endingness of this battle isn't limited to this one mitzvah — it's what it means to be a Jew.

Let me clarify.

First of all, it's true that *tznius* specifically can be a very, very over-whelming mitzvah. You can get lost in all of the details to the point that suddenly you stop and ask yourself, What on earth am I doing? This all makes no sense! It cannot be that the elbow, knee, collarbone, tap on the shoulder, phone call, comment is that big a deal. Does Hashem really care if I...? Really?!

So, first of all, I hope at this point you realize that the vastness of this particular mitzvah is directly related to the import it has on the Jewish people. The reason why schools, parents, etc. seem to be so fix-ated on this issue is because they understand (please tell me you do a little bit too. Please.) that our *tznius* guards our *kedushah* guards our everything. Like I keep saying — *tznius* is not about the elbow or the second piercing. It's about a decision one makes toward which direc-tion one is facing: *kedushah* or *pritzus*. Stop seeing things in such an extreme way i.e. "It cannot be that if one has a boyfriend, her *berachos* has no meaning." Right, duh, obviously. The positive decisions you make in *tznius* make you beautiful, special, holy. When you slip up in some, well, so goes life. You pick yourself up and try again.

You know, I don't think you guys have a clue how incredible you are. Out of the billions of people on the planet, G-d chose the Jews to be His people and spread His word. And out of those millions of Jews, there are only a fraction who actually follow His commandments. And out of that fraction, only a very small amount think about and struggle with doing what He wants us to be doing, as opposed to just going through the motions. You are included in that small amount. I don't care where you are holding in your *frumkeit* or your *tznius*, the fact that you are thinking and taking it seriously means you're doing exactly what you're supposed to be doing. Hashem wants a fighting Jew, not a perfect Jew, so even when you fail, go down fighting.

Sometimes it's really hard to be a Jew. The *halachos* are endless, the details intense and the requirements are totally draining — and often just boring.

I hate cooking. I hate that I'm in charge of the shopping and cleaning and laundry and carpooling and diaper changing and I never even liked little kids. Sometimes at the end of the day I'm too tired to find my bed — then I get up at night ten times for drinks and kisses and sometimes just to say hi and start it all again the next day. Then I speak to my friend who does not yet have children and the loneliness and emptiness scare me out of my mind and I'm overwhelmed with happiness at my life. It's not that I suddenly love the housekeeping; it's just that I'm better able to put it into the context of perfect, healthy children and husband.

To be a mother and a wife is not about washing dishes — though that must get done, as *tznius* is not about covering your knees — though that must get done, as to be a Jew is not about eating kosher — though that must get done. To be a mother and a wife is to know what it is to give and love; to live with *tznius* is to live with *kedushah* and sanctity; to be a Jew is to be one of G-d's chosen nation, destined for eternal joy in this world and the World to Come.

Still with me? Sorry so heavy, but your journals don't really make for easy reading, either. Keep writing and give me some encouragement about these meetings — I could use some right now.

Mrs. Goldin

• • •

So... when was the last time you guys went shopping for clothes? Can you write about it?

Mrs. Goldin

• • •

Guys —

First of all — about the journals: stop obsessing about what you're writing — is it enough, is it stupid, is it what I want...this whole thing is totally about you and your thoughts — not about me! I don't comment often, not because I don't like what you're writing — only because I don't want to be an influence on your journals. So far you're all doing great.

Try to sit down once a week to record any thoughts you might have about *tznius*. Tell me if there's anything that doesn't make sense to you or that you're uncomfortable with. Have our meetings been affecting the way you act/dress at all? (Specifics please.) How about the way you see other people's actions/dress? Which issues in *tznius* are still difficult for you? Which have become less difficult? What will make a difference to you in this area?

I have absolutely no idea what I meant with that last question, scratch it.

Keep this list of questions handy and please keep writing, writing, writing. I know you're all so busy with so many other things, but this is important. In five years, your words might really mean a lot to some kid struggling with these concepts. Imagine that!

See you next time.

Mrs. Goldin

P.S. Feel free to call me with any questions in between meetings.

Oh, one more thing — I was listening to the recording of the last meeting and I feel like I put way too much of an emphasis on looking beautiful. Please don't misunderstand me. I didn't mean to make it sound like it's an *aveirah* if you don't look pretty — it's not. I just meant that I feel strongly that as Daughters of the King, especially as those who know and try to live by the rules of *tznius*, we have the added responsibility of looking nice. I want people to point a finger at you guys and say — see, it *is* possible to be cool/pretty/nice looking and *tznius* at the same time. Is that too much to ask?

I don't know, tell me — is it?

• • •

Ok.

I know things are really intense for you these days because of midterms and all, but this is our last note before midwinter. Things are going to be changing a bit after that — I'm going to keep you posted when you come back to school. In any case, I just wanted to remind you to take along your journals wherever you're going for vacation and keep them updated. Also, can we try not to write exclusively about boys? I mean it's totally fine, but keep in mind that *tznius* is about much, much more.

Ever saw someone wearing very heavy makeup? Can this be appropriate in some places and not in others? Could dancing fall under the category of *tznius*? (Calm down, you know I'm not talking about any and all dancing.) What if there are only girls around? Does the fact that there are no guys make everything ok? I'm just wondering.

Good luck on your midterms, but between me and you — your journals measure your progress more accurately. You're all great.

Mrs. Goldin

• • •

Hey —

So here are your journals back. You know, I stand in awe of all of you. Not because I think you're so great (so get over yourselves), just because you're all so real. Keep pushing yourselves.

Can you write about *tznius* and language? What about in the topics you discuss with your friends? Do you feel that it is way above your level to think about these things?

Also, do you guys know what *bushah* is? Do you know that it's one of three uniquely Jewish traits? And that Rav Dessler says that it is extremely easily suffocated. But we really need to talk about that in person.

How would you feel about reading parts of your journals out loud to each other? Yeah, I know, but I think it would be helpful. Push your comfort zone, guys — let that be your motto in all things. We'll talk.

Mrs. Goldin

• • •

Guys —

First of all sorry, but Wednesday doesn't work for me in the end, so cancel that and I'll let you know when we're going to reschedule. I realize that a lot of you are running dry on what to write — I know. I also don't care, keep writing. Look at your closet, look at your friends, look at your mom (ok, leave her out), and write. Think about *tznius* in terms of things other than dress — like speech, action, attitude — and write.

Okay question of the week — everyone has certain red lines which they wouldn't cross in every area of Judaism. What are your red lines — the borders you've drawn for yourself — in *tznius*? What would you absolutely not buy/wear? How did you come up with these criteria? Your parents? Yourselves? Is there anything which is halachically okay, but you still wouldn't wear/ don't fit your standards of *tznius*?

And how was school Shabbos?

Have a great week guys! I'll keep you posted about the meeting.

Mrs. Goldin

• • •

So...don't know if you guys have noticed, but the weather is warmer. Write about it.

• • •

Okay —
Last topic before Pesach:

How has keeping this journal affected your growth? (I know it's kinda obvious, but I want you to write about it anyway).

Have a great *yom yov*. Keep being awesome, I'll see you soon.

Mrs. Goldin

• • •

So,

We're kind of down to the count at this point. We will be meeting twice more, so start looking back over these letters and make sure you've addressed all of my questions.

How has working on *tznius* affected the people around you? Did they react in any way?

As the year is winding down I know you're flooded with school work, but please keep writing. Think about topics that you would love to read about.

See you in two weeks,

Mrs. Goldin

• • •

Wow. Last letter.

Okay — I'm collecting your journals next week, the day after Shavuos — no exceptions!

This week's topic: How have you changed over this past year? (You knew this was coming). Be specific:

How have your thoughts about *tznius* changed?

Your clothing and actions?

Your perceptions of others?

And anything else. Be clear in your "before" and "afters" and try not to be vague and/or cliched, (as in 'now I understand the meaning of blah, blah, blah...' It may be true, but teenagers will not want to hear that type of thing. I think.).

See you next week guys — I'm looking forward.

Mrs. Goldin

Appendix B

In all areas of *avodas Hashem*, prayer — asking Hashem for His help in our struggles and challenges — is essential for our success. The following is an example of a personal *bakashah*, asking for *siyatta diShmaya* in the area of *tznius*. As with any request, each person can use her own words and tailor her prayer to her own needs.

רבונו של עולם, אנא רחום וחנון, זכני שאהיה בת ישראל כשרה
וצנועה כרצונך, והסר כל המפריעים לעבודתך, אנא השם, אתה
המסייע להבאים להטהר ואתה אמרת "פתחו לי פתח כחודו של
מחט ואני אפתח לכם פתח כפתחו של אולם" הנה אני עשכיו
פותחת לך, אבי שבשמים, פתח כחודו של מחט ומתחננת לפניך.
אנא השם, אני רוצה לשוב אליך בתשובה שלמה וללכת בצניעות,
אבל קשה לי, יש לי הרבה נסיונות ומפריעים, לך לא קשה שום
דבר, תעזור לי להתגבר בשמחה על כל הנסיונות ותסלק מהר את
כל המפריעים ואזכה להיות יהודי' כשרה כרצונך, השטה ושמחה
מאוד בקיום התורה הקדושה. ויהי רצון מלפניך שלא יכשלו בי בני
אדם, אנא השם, רחום וחנון, רחם עלי ועזור לי ושמע תפילתי כי
אתה שומע תפילה. ברוך שומע תפילה.

MRS. ALIZA GOLDIN grew up in Brooklyn and lives in New Jersey with her husband and children. She has been teaching, running programs and speaking to teenage girls for the past ten years. She can be reached at 6diaries@kewnet.com.